Gladstone Christian Church
305 E. Dartmouth
Gladstone, OR 97027

THE LAYMAN'S BIBLE COMMENTARY

THE LAYMAN'S BIBLE COMMENTARY
IN TWENTY-FIVE VOLUMES

THE LAYMAN'S
BIBLE COMMENTARY

Balmer H. Kelly, *Editor*

Donald G. Miller   *Associate Editors*   Arnold B. Rhodes

Dwight M. Chalmers, *Editor,* John Knox Press

VOLUME 18

THE GOSPEL ACCORDING TO
LUKE

Donald G. Miller

JOHN KNOX PRESS

ATLANTA, GEORGIA

10 9 8 7 6 5 4 3 2

Complete set: ISBN: 0-8042-3086-2
This volume: 0-8042-3078-1
Library of Congress Card Number: 59-10454
First paperback edition 1982
Printed in the United States of America
John Knox Press
Atlanta, Georgia 30365

PREFACE

The LAYMAN'S BIBLE COMMENTARY is based on the conviction that the Bible has the Word of good news for the whole world. The Bible is not the property of a special group. It is not even the property and concern of the Church alone. It is given to the Church for its own life but also to bring God's offer of life to all mankind—wherever there are ears to hear and hearts to respond.

It is this point of view which binds the separate parts of the LAYMAN'S BIBLE COMMENTARY into a unity. There are many volumes and many writers, coming from varied backgrounds, as is the case with the Bible itself. But also as with the Bible there is a unity of purpose and of faith. The purpose is to clarify the situations and language of the Bible that it may be more and more fully understood. The faith is that in the Bible there is essentially one Word, one message of salvation, one gospel.

The LAYMAN'S BIBLE COMMENTARY is designed to be a concise non-technical guide for the layman in personal study of his own Bible. Therefore, no biblical text is printed along with the comment upon it. This commentary will have done its work precisely to the degree in which it moves its readers to take up the Bible for themselves.

The writers have used the Revised Standard Version of the Bible as their basic text. Occasionally they have differed from this translation. Where this is the case they have given their reasons. In the main, no attempt has been made either to justify the wording of the Revised Standard Version or to compare it with other translations.

One objective in this commentary is to provide the most helpful explanation of fundamental matters in simple up-to-date terms. Exhaustive treatment of subjects has not been undertaken.

In our age knowledge of the Bible is perilously low. At the same time there are signs that many people are longing for help in getting such knowledge. Knowledge of and about the Bible is, of course, not enough. The grace of God and the work of the Holy Spirit are essential to the renewal of life through the Scriptures. It is in the happy confidence that the great hunger for the Word is a sign of God's grace already operating within men, and that the Spirit works most wonderfully where the Word is familiarly known, that this commentary has been written and published.

THE EDITORS AND
THE PUBLISHERS

THE GOSPEL ACCORDING TO

LUKE

INTRODUCTION

The Nature of the Gospel

Luke's Gospel is *gospel*—"good news"—not biography. It must, therefore, be read not as a "life of Jesus" but as a message of what God has done for us in him.

The nature of Luke's Gospel is indicated by the role of those from whom he got his materials. They were "ministers of the word" (1:2). They were heralds of the "good news" of what God had done for them in Jesus. It was their aim to retell some of Jesus' sayings and doings in such a way that those to whom they told them would likewise find God. The materials of Luke's Gospel, therefore, were first of all *preached*.

This means that if the depths of this Gospel are to be plumbed, it will be by the response of *faith*. A testimony to faith is designed to awaken faith. And only through faith can such testimony be understood. At this point the peculiar nature of the "good news" of the gospel is clear. It confronts the reader with historic events, but the value lies in what the events mean for faith. The gospel is not basically a set of religious ideas. It is the record of what God has *done* for man. As in the Old Testament, so in the New, the Word of the Lord "happened." Yet the events themselves were insufficient apart from faith. Before the events could become "good news," those who saw them, or heard about them, were under the necessity of believing that God was acting in them for the salvation of man. Multitudes who saw Jesus, conversed with him, and had no problem whatsoever about what happened as historic event, still rejected him. They did not deny his deeds. But what was the source of them? God, or Satan? Was he to be despised as a fanatic, admired as a hero, or worshiped as divine? *"And they crucified him."*

Luke writes facts that are God's "good news." They must be studied as such. This demands intellectual effort and honesty. But beyond that it requires faith, surrender, obedience, service, worship. Here Life speaks to life, and must be answered by life.

The Purpose

The book is dedicated to one called "most excellent Theophilus" (1:3). Theophilus is a Greek name, strongly suggesting that the man was a Gentile. The title "most excellent" hints that he was a person of high rank (see Acts 23:26; 24:2). It was customary in Luke's day, as in ours, to dedicate to an individual a book intended for a much wider group. Theophilus, however, would be representative of this group, which must have been composed of Gentiles of high intelligence and culture. This is confirmed by the style of Luke's preface (1:1-4). It is written in the literary form of secular Greek historians, and has a quality of language which reveals the author to have been a man of learning. Thus it seems clear that Luke was deliberately setting out to present the Christian message in a form which would capture the attention of the intelligent Gentile mind of the first century.

Theophilus himself knew something of the Christian faith. Luke addresses him as one who has been "informed" (1:4). This is the root of our word "catechized." Whether Theophilus had been formally catechized, which the word strongly suggests (see Acts 18:25; I Cor. 14:19; Gal. 6:6, where the same Greek word is used), or whether his information about the faith was less formal, it is difficult to say. In any case, he knows something about Christianity, but is still in need of fuller knowledge of its content and fuller trust in its authenticity.

What would lead an informed Gentile of the seventh or eighth decade of the first century to question Christianity? Two living issues faced him. First, the growing cult of Emperor-worship in the Roman Empire offered salvation to men through the Roman Caesar. The emperor was called "savior," "son of God," and "Lord and God." Men were to live before him in "fear" and "peace." He would usher in the "golden age." In consequence of this, stories were circulated about miracles which the emperors allegedly performed. Augustus was reported to have made withered trees come to life and to have healed the sick. Hadrian allegedly produced rain in parched Africa. Of Domitian it was told that wild animals would not harm him. Elephants did obeisance to him. The moon and stars stood still in order to get a longer look at him. His dealings were thought of as divine deeds. His pardon was actually called "gospel," the identical word used in the New Testament for the Christian gospel.

With the spread of this Emperor-worship, what was Luke's task? It was so to present the story of Jesus that an intelligent Gentile sincerely seeking salvation would discover the goal of his search in Jesus, not in Caesar. So Luke sets Jesus' birth in relation to Caesar Augustus (2:1), and connects the beginning of his public ministry with the reign of Tiberius Caesar (3:1). Luke's Gospel is the rehearsal of Jesus' words and deeds in such fashion that the earliest Christian creed would be authenticated: "Jesus Christ is Lord" (Phil. 2:11; Rom. 10:9; 14:9). It brought to the fore the issue which later led to persecution of the Christians, whether Caesar or Jesus was the Lord of the whole world, and confronted the reader with a decision.

The second issue faced by the Gentile world in an honest look at Christianity lay in the discrediting of Judaism in the latter half of the first century. The strife between Jew and Gentile was an ever-rising crescendo. In A.D. 49 Claudius decreed that all Jews should be banished from Rome. In the year 66 a persecution broke out in Alexandria which annihilated 50,000 Jews. Similar events took place in other cities. Pagan writers scorned the Jews as an ancient slave people, still no better than slaves. Jewish customs were ridiculed, Jewish worship was blasphemed. This was all climaxed in the Jewish War of A.D. 66-70. Jerusalem was captured. The Temple was destroyed. The Jewish people were driven out into the world as defenseless sheep without a shepherd.

The problem raised by all this for the Gentile mind was: Christianity obviously came out of Judaism. If Judaism is discredited, does Christianity fall with it? Luke's aim was to answer this question with an emphatic, No. This involved a difficult theological question faced by both Jew and Gentile in the Early Church. If Jesus were truly the Messiah, why did the accredited Jewish leaders reject him? This problem is faced by Luke both in the Gospel and in the Acts (Luke 24:20; Acts 2:23; 7:52-53; 13:44-47; 28:24-28). Luke insists that their rejection did not thwart the purpose of God nor invalidate the Christian faith. In fact, the shattering of first-century Judaism was the authentication of the Christian faith. It was God's judgment on the Jews' failure to realize the nature of their own mission. Christianity, on the other hand, was the real heir of the Old Testament faith.

Distinguishing Characteristics

Luke was a friend and pupil of the Apostle Paul. Many of the special traits of his Gospel, therefore, bear the marks of that relationship. Luke did not use Paul's characteristic words, nor rewrite the "good news" to fit Paul's thought. Yet in his selection of materials and the way he used them, he shows that the truths which Paul proclaimed were not novel ideas, but were rooted in the life and teaching of Jesus himself.

The Universality of the Gospel

Perhaps the most marked characteristic of Luke's Gospel is its emphasis on the universality of the Christian faith. From beginning to end it is clear that in Christ "there is neither Jew nor Greek" (Gal. 3:28). From Simeon's song about Jesus being "a light . . . to the Gentiles" (2:32), to the last encounter of the risen Lord with his disciples, when he told them that "repentance and forgiveness of sins should be preached in his name to *all nations*" (24:47), Luke emphasized the fact that the gospel is not for Jews only but for all peoples. The central theme is that *Jesus is the Savior of the whole world*.

In order to reinforce this message, Luke omitted much that was purely Jewish in character. For example, he omits the materials in Matthew's Sermon on the Mount which deal directly with Jesus' relation to the Jewish law (Matt. 5:21-48; 6:1-8, 16-18). The stress on Jesus' battle with the scribes and Pharisees is less marked than in Matthew (Luke omits Matthew 23, for example). The discussion in Mark 7:1-23 over the Jewish tradition about ceremonial cleanness is lacking in Luke.

Furthermore, Luke included much of a positively universal nature. More than the other Gospel writers, he related his story to events of the Roman Empire (2:1-2; 3:1). He wanted to show that what he was writing has meaning for every man, that Jesus is Lord even of world empire. The baby Jesus lying in the arms of old Simeon in the Temple is spoken of as "a light for revelation to the Gentiles" (2:32). Luke traces Jesus' ancestry not, as does Matthew, from Abraham down, but follows it all the way back to Adam, showing that Jesus is related not only to the sons of Abraham but to every man who was ever born (3:23-38). These touches, coupled with Luke's omission of Jesus' instructions to the Twelve to "go nowhere among the Gentiles, and enter no town of the Samaritans, but go rather to the lost sheep of the house of Israel" (Matt. 10:5-6; see also Matt. 15:24), are Luke's way of tracing the universal mission of the Church back to Jesus himself.

All this, too, must be considered in the light of Luke's second volume, The Acts, where the story gathers around the broadening mission of the Church from Jerusalem to Rome. In the light of her great struggle with Jewish exclusiveness (see Acts 15 and Gal. 2), Luke in his Gospel is showing that the Church's mission to the whole world sprang originally from the mind of Jesus, bound by no ties of nation, race, culture, or tradition. It was God's "good news" to all the world.

The Gospel and the Samaritans

A special feature of the universality of Luke's Gospel is the large place it gives to the Samaritans. On both political and religious grounds, the Samaritans were considered outside the pale of fellowship by the Jews of Jesus' day. In contrast to this attitude, Luke shows Jesus working among the Samaritans (9:51-56; 17:11). In the parable of the Good Samaritan (10:25-37) and the story of the Samaritan leper who was healed (17:11-19), Jesus singled out the Samaritans as examples of true neighborliness and gratitude. They were nearer the Kingdom than many of the self-righteous Jews who would have shut them out.

Why this emphasis on the Samaritans? The answer lies in the history of the Early Church. The opposition which Philip's mission to the Samaritans must have stirred up (Acts 8), and Luke's use of this mission to introduce the conversion of Saul—around whom the controversy later raged over taking the gospel to the Gentiles (Acts 15)—give point to Luke's stress here. He was showing that the Samaritan mission was rooted in the mind of Jesus.

In stressing the universality of the gospel, however, Luke is in no way anti-Semitic. He underlines the fact that Jesus is rooted in Judaism. He alone reports the circumcision and dedication of Jesus (2:21-24), and his visit to the Temple at the age of twelve (2:41-52). Luke alone tells of the pious Jews such as Simeon and Anna, Zechariah and Elizabeth, who were the faithful remnant of the Jews "looking for the consolation of Israel," upon whom the Holy Spirit rested (2:25). Throughout his Gospel, Luke shows how Jesus was the fulfillment of the Old Testament story of salvation, who can be understood only in the light of the Law, the Prophets, and the Psalms (see 24:25-27, 44-47).

The Gospel and the Lost

In the light of his purpose to present Jesus as the Savior of all sorts of men, Luke places special emphasis on Jesus' love for the ones whom the world considers outcasts. In fact, it is only those who know that they are lost who can know his mercy.

This feature can be clearly seen in the light of the materials Luke uses which are not given in the other Gospels. These include the following: the story of the Pharisee and the sinful woman (7:36-50); the parables of the Lost Sheep, the Lost Coin, and the Lost Son (15:1-32); the parable of the Pharisee and the Publican (18:9-14); the story of Zacchaeus (19:1-10); the pardon of the thief on the cross (23:39-43); and the special appearance of the risen Lord to Peter (24:34), whose only claim to Jesus' attention was that he had confessed himself to be "a sinful man" (5:8) and had denied him (22:31-34, 54-62). This special feature of Luke's Gospel shows in Jesus the roots of the theology which Paul later developed: "when the goodness and loving kindness of God our Savior appeared, he saved us, not because of deeds done by us in righteousness, but in virtue of his own mercy . . . so that we might be justified by his grace" (Titus 3:4-7).

The Gospel and the Poor

Of all the Gospels, Luke gives the most prominence to Jesus' warnings about the danger of riches and his special compassion for the poor. Luke alone lists the vivid warnings against the danger of covetousness and riches which are contained in the parable of the Rich Fool who tried to feed his soul on "possessions" (12:13-21), the story of the rich man's indifference to poverty-stricken Lazarus (16:19-31), and Zacchaeus' decision to give half of his goods to the poor (19:1-10). He alone records Jesus' counsel to "sell your possessions, and give alms" (12:33), and his encouragement to "invite the poor" to dinner (14:13). All of this emphasis is an outgrowth of God's regard for the poor in the gift of his Son, over whose coming Mary sings, "he has filled the hungry with good things, and the rich he has sent empty away" (1:53).

In this way Luke related the teaching of Jesus to the problem of materialism which was widely discussed in the Gentile world of the first century. There were philosophers called Stoics who scorned wealth and taught that men should be indifferent to money. Their reason for this, however, was very different from that of Jesus. For the Stoics, dependence on wealth was unworthy of the human personality. For Jesus it was wrong because it pushed God from the center of life, and thus became idolatrous. Again, Luke's materials root in the mind of Jesus the thought of Paul, who defined covetousness as "idolatry" (Col. 3:5), and called the "love of money" the "root of all evils," the craving for which leads men "away from the faith" (I Tim. 6:10).

The Gospel and Womanhood

Another special characteristic of Luke's Gospel is the prominence given to women. In contrast to Matthew, where the birth story centers in Joseph and his problem, Luke focuses his attention on Mary. Peculiar to Luke is the story of the prophetess, Anna (2:36-38); the dealing of Jesus with the sinful woman (7:36-50) and the woman with an eighteen-year infirmity (13: 11-13); the relation of Jesus to Mary and Martha (10:38-42); and two parables in which women are the central characters (15: 8-10; 18:1-8). Besides, Luke also includes items about women told elsewhere, but gives more detail (8:2). This attention given to women fits in well with Luke's purpose to offer Jesus to the Gentiles. The emancipation of women was more advanced among the Gentiles than among the Jews in the first century, yet at the same time there was greater degradation of pagan women. Luke was tracing directly to Jesus Paul's doctrine that in Christ "there is neither male nor female" (Gal. 3:28).

The Holy Spirit and Prayer

Luke gives more stress than the other Gospels to the work of the Holy Spirit, both in the life of Jesus and in the continuing witness of the Church. He mentions the activity of the Holy Spirit in the pious folk from whom John the Baptist and Jesus had their origin (1:35, 41, 67; 2:25). Jesus' public career is begun "in the power of the Spirit" (4:14), and he interprets his mission through the words of the prophet, "The Spirit of the Lord is upon me" (4:18). In Jesus' teaching on prayer, Luke changes Matthew's "good things" to "the Holy Spirit" which the Father gives in response to prayer (Matt. 7:11; Luke 11:13). In preparation for the later account of the Holy Spirit at Pentecost (Acts 2), Luke records Jesus' instructions to the disciples to "stay in the city, until you are clothed with power from on high" (24:49).

Hand in hand with this emphasis goes that on the importance of prayer. Luke alone connects prayer with Jesus' baptism (3:21), his calling of the Twelve (6:12), the Great Confession (9:18), the Transfiguration (9:28), and the denial of Peter (22: 31-34). He also connects the giving of the Lord's Prayer with Jesus' own praying (11:1-4), and records the parable of the Unjust Judge (18:1-8) and that of the Pharisee and the Publican (18:9-14), both of which have prayer as their center. Once again Luke stands close to Paul, whose counsel was to use "the sword of the Spirit" and to "pray at all times" (Eph. 6:17-18).

The Author

The Gospel according to Luke carries no direct statement about who wrote it. There are many clear indications, however, that it was written by the one whose name it now bears: Luke, the doctor companion of Paul. There is a very old and very widespread tradition among the Early Church Fathers which links his name with this work. Furthermore, there is no rival tradition. Either Luke wrote it or the Early Church left us no hint whatever of its author. If Luke did not write it, it is difficult to see how the tradition arose which connected his name with it, inasmuch as he is too obscure a character in the New Testament to have had his name attached purely by accident to this Gospel and to the Book of the Acts. If the evidences within the work do not weigh against it, the early, unanimous tradition of Lukan authorship would seem to be well founded.

In examining the problem of authorship from within the work itself, the argument rests more heavily on the Acts than on the Gospel. Although it has been challenged, it is almost universally accepted that Luke and the Acts are two volumes from one pen. Whoever wrote the Acts wrote also the Gospel.

What evidences are there for Lukan authorship of the Acts? There are in the Acts three sections in which the writer abruptly turns from the third person and reports the events in the first person. These are the so-called "we-passages" (Acts 16:10-17; 20:5—21:18; 27:1—28:16). The use of the first person indicates that the author himself participated in the events described, and was a companion of Paul on those occasions. But did the friend of Paul who wrote these sections also write the whole work? On the basis of the words he uses, his literary style, and his theological outlook, it has been established as firmly as is possible in such matters that the entire Book of Acts came from the hand of the writer of the "we-passages." The author of the Acts, then, was one of Paul's companions who was with him at the time of the events described in the first person. Of the few Gentiles mentioned by Paul in his letters written during the period when the writer of the Acts was with him, Luke is the most likely one to have written it. If Luke wrote the Acts, he also wrote the Gospel.

Does what we know of Luke accord with this judgment? We know that he was a Gentile, for Paul lists him among his Gentile friends (Col. 4:14; see Col. 4:11). We know that he was a doctor, for Paul calls him "the beloved physician" (Col. 4:14). We know that he was with Paul during at least a part of the period covered by the "we-passages" in Acts (Philemon 24; Col. 4:14; II Tim. 4:11), and that he stood by him to the end (II Tim. 4:11). We have already seen that the Gospel was written by a Gentile, and that the writer was loyal to Paul's theology. It has also been cogently argued that the Gospel was written by a physician. Although the argument falls short of proof and has been severely challenged, it is still clear that there is nothing in the work that a physician could not have written, and in comparing the healing-stories with those of Matthew and Mark, the presumption grows that the Gospel came from the pen of a doctor. Luke fulfills the requirements for being the author of the Gospel.

In the light of all this, which accords well with the unanimous tradition of the Early Church, although Lukan authorship may fall just short of indisputable proof, the evidence for it is quite strong enough, save for those of the most skeptical turn of mind.

Place and Date

Both tradition and Luke's precise knowledge of the church at Antioch connect him with that city (Acts 6:5; 11:19-26; 13: 1-3; 14:26-28; 15:1-35). This does not mean, however, that he wrote either *from* there or *to* there. He may have written to the church at Rome or to one of the churches in Greece. The exact place from which or to which he wrote remains uncertain. A like uncertainty prevails as to when he wrote. The one precise date in early Christianity is the fall of Jerusalem, in A.D. 70. Some see hints in Luke's Gospel that Jerusalem had already fallen, whereas others likewise see strong hints that it was still standing when Luke wrote. The evidence is too precarious to be decisive. The earliest date suggested is around A.D. 60, the latest is A.D. 95. By far the largest number of scholars feel that the preferable date is sometime between A.D. 70 and 80. Fortunately, the worth of the Gospel for us in no way rests on this point.

OUTLINE

COMMENTARY

PREFACE
Luke 1:1-4

Luke helps us greatly in the understanding of his Gospel by the information he gives in his preface. In this one sentence of four verses, written in the best classic style of his day, Luke tells us several significant things. First, he mentions the *occasion* of his writing. "Inasmuch as many have undertaken to compile a narrative" (vs. 1), he, too, has decided to produce one. It was a period when there were a good many attempts to set down written records of the life and ministry of Jesus. This was necessary for several reasons. The gospel was initially preached by those who had been with Jesus from the first (Acts 1:21-22). Their time and effort were given to spreading the story by word of mouth. As the Church began to grow, and to advance rapidly throughout the Roman Empire far from the Holy Land, there were not enough eyewitnesses of all that Jesus did and taught to be in every place. This necessitated the beginning of collections of stories about him, especially the Passion story, and groups of teachings which could be used for preaching and for instruction of new converts. Then, too, as the years went by, some of the Apostles were martyred (Acts 12:1-2), and others were nearing death through old age. It was imperative that their memories of Jesus should be recorded for future generations. Furthermore, as the Church in various places faced difficult problems, it was natural that there should be searched out and recorded those things about Jesus which were helpful in solving these problems. Hence, the first period of oral transmission of the story gave way to the second period of fragmentary collections of Jesus' deeds and words. The third stage naturally followed this. In order to equip the Church more adequately for missionary and instructional work, these fragmentary collections were assembled by various writers into a more ordered and complete story. It was at this third stage that Luke began his work. He makes no judgment on others who were drawing up a narrative, for he includes himself in this group—"it seemed good to me also" (vs. 3). He feels, however, that no one of these stories is quite adequate for the special purpose he had in mind. Hence, he, too, took up the task.

The *subject matter* of Luke's Gospel is "the things which have been accomplished among us" (vs. 1). This means that Luke is not primarily offering a set of religious ideas, nor a philosophy of life he has worked out, nor advice on how to succeed and be happy. He is primarily telling things that *happened*. Gospel means "good news," and news is always about something that has taken place. The heart of Luke's story, then, is the glorious news of what God has done for us in Jesus Christ. The word "accomplished" carries with it the idea of certainty, full persuasion, conviction (see Rom. 4:21; 14:5). Luke's subject matter involves well-attested events in which God is the chief actor.

The strongest attestation of these events is the existence of the community which they brought into being. "The things which have been accomplished *among us*," says Luke. That involves a group, a community of faith, a Church, created by the power of the events to which this Gospel bears witness. Luke's subject matter, therefore, is not something he has concocted. It is rather the voice of the whole community of faith, bearing witness to that which had brought it into being and now sustained its life.

Since Luke came into the Christian Church long after Jesus died, he had to depend on other *sources* of information for his story. Those from whom he got his material he describes as "eyewitnesses and ministers of the word" (vs. 2). His informants were authenticated by two facts. First, they were "eyewitnesses." They had been with Jesus himself and had seen with their own eyes the things they told. Second, their witness was confirmed by the fact that they had given their lives to the service of him about whom they spoke. They were "ministers." This does not mean that they were clergymen. The word "minister" literally means one who rows under the command of another. It came, then, to mean one who serves the interests of another, whose function it is to carry out the will of a superior. Those who "delivered" the story to Luke corroborated it by enthroning Jesus as Lord.

What Luke's sources were can be partially determined from his Gospel. It is quite generally agreed that one of them was the Gospel by Mark. (If Mark was not an eyewitness, his Gospel is based on the preaching of Peter, and thus contains eyewitness reports.) Luke has used more than half of Mark's Gospel (356 out of 661 verses), and has followed his general plan of arrangement. The other materials he uses are inserted into Mark's plan.

Besides this large use of Mark, Luke has about 235 verses,

mainly the teachings of Jesus, which are found also in Matthew's
Gospel. Luke's free rearrangement of the order of these mate-
rials, however, suggests that he did not take them directly from
Matthew, but took them from an unknown source which he and
Matthew used in common. These materials are usually known by
the symbol "Q," the first letter of the German word for "source."

Almost half of Luke's Gospel (about 548 out of 1149 verses)
is unique, and included in this are some of the most cherished
materials we possess. It is impossible to determine where Luke
got these materials. According to Acts, Luke was with Paul when
he arrived in Jerusalem for the last time. Furthermore, he was
with him two years later when he sailed from Caesarea, as a prisoner, to Rome. (Acts 21:17 and 27:1 are both "we-passages,"
as discussed in the Introduction.) Where Luke was during that
two-year period is not known, but the probability is that he spent
the time near Paul in the neighborhood of Jerusalem and Caesarea, for he seems to have adopted a permanent policy of staying
near Paul (II Tim. 4:11). During this period he would have had
ample opportunity to visit with countless people who were eyewitnesses of the life of our Lord. It may well be that in this way
he assembled the materials which he alone uses.

Luke's *method* was that of a historian. His faith did not rule
out the activity of his mind. The inspiration of the Holy Spirit
came not without intellectual toil, but through it. A more accu-
rate translation of verse 3 than that given in the Revised Standard Version would be, "having traced the course of all things
accurately from the beginning." The word "follow" or "trace"
means to follow someone so closely that he is never out of sight.
The pursuit of a detective or the careful watching of a bodyguard
suggests the diligence with which Luke traced the origin and de-
velopment of the story he was about to write. The result of this
careful search is better suggested by the reading in the margin,
"accurately." He has satisfied himself as to the "accuracy" or re-
liability of all that he tells. And not only has he done this "for
some time past," he has also traced the story back to its "beginning," back farther than any of the other Gospel writers, clear
back to the announcement of the birth of John the Baptist.

Luke had a *plan,* for he claims to be writing "an orderly
account" (vs. 3). He has selected a very scanty number of possible items that could have been told about Jesus (see John 21:
25), and has arranged them in an order which he feels will best

serve the purpose which he has in mind for his readers. The order, then, is less chronological and biographical than it is theological.

The *readers* for whom the Gospel was designed are symbolized by the one to whom the work is dedicated—Theophilus. It has been conjectured that Theophilus was not an individual, but merely a symbolic name for "Christian," since it means "lover of God." The custom of dedicating books to outstanding individuals, however, makes it likely that he was a real person. Who he was or where he lived, we do not know. From the character of the Gospel we can only conclude that Theophilus represented the intelligent Gentile seeker after truth, for whom Luke wrote.

The *purpose* which Luke sought to fulfill was that people such as Theophilus might "know the truth" concerning the things of which they had "been informed" (vs. 4). To establish the authenticity and trustworthiness of the Christian faith for seeking Gentiles was Luke's aim (see the Introduction).

THE COMING OF MESSIAH:
FULFILLMENT OF PROMISE

Luke 1:5—2:40

Two events are interwoven here: the birth of John the Baptist and the birth of Jesus. Luke intends to suggest that in these two events and what flowed from them, a new epoch began in human history. This was not only a *new* epoch, but the *decisive* epoch of all history. As history had its beginning in the creation of "the heavens and the earth" (Gen. 1:1), here is the beginning of the saving process whereby God is to create "new heavens and a new earth in which righteousness dwells" (II Peter 3:13; see also Isa. 65:17 and Rev. 21:1).

This section has been called the "Gospel of the Infancy." The title is apt, for these stories are truly *gospel*. Throughout the whole section, like an overture to a symphony, runs the theme: *God brings salvation*. This is clearly seen in the names of the two boys whose birth is promised. "John" means "The LORD is gracious," and "Jesus" means "The LORD is salvation." In line with these names, God is the actor throughout. Man only waits, hopes, trusts, receives. Zechariah and Elizabeth are past the age when they can have a son. God does the impossible and graciously gives them a son. Mary has not known a man, yet God gives her a son. The shepherds, held in contempt because of the low economic level of their employment, are joyfully surprised at the gracious announcement of the angels. Simeon and Anna have spent their lives in one long, disappointed "looking for the consolation of Israel" (2:25, 38), but now they can give "thanks to God" (2:38), saying, "Mine eyes have seen thy salvation" (2:30). Man can only wait, hope, receive, praise. Salvation comes from God alone. *But salvation comes!* Here is "good news."

Each of the central characters in this first section is faced with the unbelievable. "How shall I know this?" asked Zechariah (1:18). "How can this be . . . ?" said Mary (1:34). "What then will this child be?" queried the people at John's birth (1:66). "Let us go over to Bethlehem and see," said the shepherds (2:15). And the people to whom they spoke "wondered at what the shepherds told them" (2:18). Simeon and Anna had spent their lives waiting for the fulfillment of a long-delayed hope. Now the unbelievable is happening—"the consolation of Israel" has come.

Is not all this designed as a fitting introduction to Luke's story? Theophilus, to whom this Gospel is dedicated, knows of the Christian faith, but needs to know the certainty of the things in which he has been instructed (1:4). Luke deftly introduces him to others who, when faced with the unbelievable "good news" about Jesus, needed certainty.

There is much in these chapters which is hard to believe. For the candid reader, however, it is the disbelief of joy (see 24:41). There are angels. There are miraculous births. There is singing in the heavens. There is prophecy. There are songs among men. The supernatural is written large across the face of these stories. This could all be shrugged off with a sophisticated air. But the thoughtful reader will ask himself: Why should it not be so? If the Spirit of God, who "in the beginning" moved over the face of the waters to bring created order out of chaos (Gen. 1:2), was again active to create a new world of righteousness in the midst of broken humanity, is it surprising that miraculous things should happen? Would it not be more surprising if they did not?

Note how sober and controlled the supernatural element is. There is miracle here, but none of it is attributed to the human actors—no, not even to the baby Jesus himself. Other stories of Jesus' childhood, which the Church rejected, tell all sorts of marvels supposedly wrought by the baby Jesus. But here, although it is clear that Luke believes this baby to be divine, he presents him as just a baby like other babies. Heaven here breaks into earth, but the facts are sober and simple.

The background against which Luke pictures Jesus' birth is in great contrast to the event itself. The place of his birth is determined by a decree of Caesar Augustus. Augustus is emperor of the world. Men worship him and call him "savior" (see the Introduction). Here is human might at its zenith. By contrast, the babe of poor, subject parents is human weakness at its lowest. Yet Luke is hinting already what history finally confirmed: Salvation lies not in the emperor, but in the Babe! The lordship of Caesar must yield to the Lordship of Jesus.

Another feature of the background here is the Temple. Heretofore, the Temple in Jerusalem was the place where God's presence was known. It was a magnificent building, with a long and sacred history, dear to the heart of every Jew throughout the world. Jesus was brought into this magnificence as a helpless infant to be dedicated to God—just a babe among hundreds of other babes brought there yearly (2:22-38). But in Simeon's song (2:34-35), one can already sense a conflict between what the Temple then represented and the purpose of God in this child. Salvation is to come no longer through the Temple, but through the babe born in the manger. God's presence will henceforth be found in him whom the angels called "Savior" (2:11).

Thus Luke sets his story in the framework of the two great rivals of Christianity in the first century—the Roman Empire and Judaism. Jesus, not Caesar, is Lord. Salvation is in Jesus, not the Temple. With this double affirmation, Luke sends his Gospel out to the Gentile world as a call to faith.

What is the mood in which the story should be read? Subtly, but surely, Luke suggests this to the reader. Of Zechariah we are told that he "did not believe" (1:20). Mary, on the other hand, is "blessed" because she "believed" (1:45). Does not this striking contrast, introduced at the very beginning of the story, suggest that the mood in which the Gospel is to be pondered is one of *faith*? It is Luke's way of putting what Jesus said to Thomas: As you examine the evidence, "do not be faithless, but believing" (John 20:27). Another element of a proper mood is to be seen in the circle of those to whom the "good news" came. They were simple-hearted, devout people, "righteous before God" (1:6), "looking for the consolation of Israel" (2:25) and "the redemp-

tion of Jerusalem" (2:38). To the devout the deepest mysteries
of life are revealed. Therefore, let the reading of the story be accompanied by *devoutness*. "Blessed are the pure in heart, for
they shall see God" (Matt. 5:8). Furthermore, read the story
with a *will to face the evidence*. The shepherds, surprised by angels, might well have turned away from their message, either because they thought it an idle tale or because they feared to pursue anything so frighteningly supernatural. Instead, they said,
"Let us go . . . and see" (2:15). To the reader who ponders
Luke's entire story in this threefold mood, the end of the way is
the road to Emmaus, where he stands in holy awe with the two
travelers who exclaimed: "Did not our hearts burn within us
while he talked to us on the road?" (24:32).

Promise of Forerunner's Birth (1:5-25)

Luke tantalizes us with his date. "In the days of Herod, king
of Judea" (1:5). Herod reigned from 37 to 4 B.C. Exactly when
during this period did this happen? Luke is more interested in the
meaning of what he describes than in precise dates. (Although
the exact date of Jesus' birth is unknown, it was several years
prior to the year A.D. 1. This discrepancy came about through a
mistake in revising the Christian calendar in the sixth century.)

John the Baptist stemmed from an old priestly line on both
sides of the house (vs. 5). "Righteous before God" is not meant
in an absolute sense (vs. 6). "Walking in all the commandments
. . . blameless," indicates that the righteousness of John's parents
was that of devout Old Testament folk who took God's Law seriously and sought to obey his known commandments. They were
still in need of the "righteousness of God" which is "apart from
law . . . through faith in Jesus Christ" (Rom. 3:21-26).

The childlessness of the couple was in no sense a punishment,
for they were well pleasing to God. It nevertheless weighed heavily on their hearts, for Elizabeth speaks of it as a "reproach"
(1:25). The Jews considered the gift of many children to be a
sign of God's blessing (Pss. 127:3-6; 128:3-4). They likewise
considered childlessness to be a sign of God's displeasure (I Sam.
1; II Sam. 6:23). One of the deepest reasons for this lay in the
fact that since ancient Israel by and large lacked a clear doctrine
of personal life after death, emphasis was placed on the belief that
a man lived on in his posterity. Thus he could share in the coming

glory of Israel, when God would fulfill his promises to her. To be childless, then, meant to be "blotted out of Israel" (Deut. 25:5-6; I Sam. 24:21), and thus to miss the future glory God had prepared for his people. Sometimes this led to the adoption of extreme measures to have children (Gen. 30:1-13; Isa. 4:1).

In their personal experience Zechariah and Elizabeth represented the bitter disappointment of generations of pious folk who were earnestly "looking for the consolation of Israel" but found it forever delayed. Ever since the return of the nation from the captivity in Babylon, more than five centuries before, hope had risen again and again, only to be beaten down. Pious living, hopeful waiting, praying—all for what? God makes good promises. But will he ever fulfill them? It was with this supreme question on his mind that Zechariah entered the Temple.

It was the priest's duty to enter the "holy place" to officiate at the altar of incense, while the people waited outside for his blessing following the offering (Exod. 30:1-8). The rising smoke of incense was associated with prayer (Ps. 141:2; Rev. 5:8; 8:3-4). Hence the people, as well as the priests, "were praying" (vs. 10). In this solemn moment, there appeared to Zechariah an angel. The position "on the right side of the altar" (vs. 11) suggests a place of honor befitting the dignity of the heavenly messenger (see 22:69; Acts 7:55; Eph. 1:20; Heb. 1:3).

Was this purely a subjective experience? It would be easy so to think. Two things, however, should be kept in mind. First, if this is just a subjective experience, it is strange, indeed, that Zechariah would believe in the reality of the experience and yet disbelieve the message it brought. Secondly, can we be sure that angels have no reality? "Angel," in the Bible, often means simply "messenger." Here, however, since the angel is later named (1: 19), it is clear that Luke means this as a real appearance of a specific angel. Can we be sure that Luke was wrong? Or can we dismiss all this as poetry? Can we be certain that God has not created intelligent beings who, in an existence quite unlike ours (20:34-36), offer him the service of perfect obedience which we men deny him? Is it not wisdom to stand reverently before the mystery of angels, assuming that we do not know enough to deny their existence, and rejoicing in the fact that God may have "many angels, numbering myriads of myriads and thousands of thousands" (Rev. 5:11), who serve him day and night, through whom more things on this earth—yes, even in our own lives—may be wrought "than this world dreams of"?

Fear was the first reaction of Zechariah to the appearance of the angel. Save for those who think God to be some sort of vague, beneficent Presence, this is not surprising. The Bible always pictures it thus (1:29-30; 2:9-10; Rev. 1:17). The approach of the holy God would be our total undoing were it not for his own gracious words, "Do not be afraid" (1:13, 30, 74; 2:10; Rev. 1:17). But we must bow before the awful majesty of his holiness in fear, before his words of grace can be spoken.

The angel's announcement to Zechariah is called "good news" —gospel! (1:19). The good news had a twofold aspect. It involved God's gracious action for the redemption of the world, and the special part that the family of Zechariah was to have in this. "Your prayer is heard," said the angel (1:13). What prayer? Hardly prayer for a son. Both Zechariah and his wife were past the age to have children (1:7, 18), and surely had ceased praying for what they now regarded as impossible. And if he had still been praying for a son, would he have objected when the angel said his prayer was answered? Furthermore, would Zechariah have been engaged in purely personal prayer in this most solemn moment of his priesthood? It is more likely that in this high hour, as Israel's representative before God, he was praying for the redemption of Israel. Then, too, had the angel's word been directed to his prayer for a son, it would have been more natural to say: "Your prayer is heard. Your wife will bear you a son." The placing of the *and* between the two parts of the sentence, however, suggests that two separate things are involved. First, your prayer for the redemption of Israel is heard. Second, as an instrument of preparing the way for this redemption, you will have a son. God offered Zechariah more than he had dared ask!

The name, manner of life, and mission of this son are all significant. John means "The LORD is gracious." Here begins God's gracious fulfillment of his promises of redemption. John will live as a Nazirite (1:15), one who is given wholly to the service of God (Num. 6:1-21; Judges 13:2-5; I Sam. 1:11). His mission is to fulfill the prophecy of Malachi with which the Old Testament ends, that one like Elijah would arise to prepare the people for the coming of the Messiah (Mal. 3:1; 4:5-6). Elijah was the prophet who, with thundering decisiveness, when the true religion well-nigh perished through the efforts of the pagan queen Jezebel, recalled Israel to faithfulness to God (I Kings 17-21).

Before Messiah came, another would arise "in the spirit and power of Elijah" to call Israel to repentance. The faithful fathers could once more look on their posterity without shame, because Israel would turn from her disobedience and become a people prepared for the Lord (1:17).

The people, waiting in the court of the Temple, wondered at Zechariah's delay. When, upon his appearing, he was unable to pronounce the priestly benediction, they knew that something unusual had taken place. Zechariah made no effort to reveal the announcement which he had received. Nor did Elizabeth. She shut herself up for five months, hiding her secret with the mystery of her husband's dumbness (a judgment on his unbelief, vs. 20), until ridicule of her hope could be silenced by her appearance (1:24-25).

This announcement of the birth of the forerunner shows us that the Old Testament was not wasted. Israel had been unfaithful. Her doom was shortly to come. Yet God worked through the remnant of the faithful in Israel to achieve his purpose. "Your prayer is heard," was God's word to this remnant (1:13).

Promise of Messiah's Birth (1:26-56)

Six months after the announcement of the birth of John, the same angel appeared to a young woman named Mary, of an obscure village of Galilee, Nazareth. Here, as before, the story is indifferent to the angel's appearance. It deals only with his mission. The greeting of the angel, "O favored one" (vs. 28), has been interpreted by the Roman Church to mean that Mary was "full of grace" which she in turn could bestow. This is an impossible interpretation. The only other place in the New Testament where this word is used it means clearly grace "bestowed" (Eph. 1:6). Mary, then, was favored not because of what she was in herself, but because the Lord was with her (vs. 28), and because she had "found favor with God" (vs. 30). She was not "mother of grace" but "daughter of grace." She was full of grace which she had received, not full of grace which she had to bestow. Mary's reply to the angel's announcement (vs. 34) clearly indicates that she was to have a son before she was married. Efforts of the Roman Church to interpret the expression, "since I have no husband," as meaning, "I never will have a husband," are out of the question. Mary is engaged to be married. Joseph refrained from marital relations only "until she had borne a son" (Matt. 1:25). Mark, Matthew, and Luke all plainly tell us that Jesus had brothers and sisters (Mark 6:3; Matt. 13:55-56; Luke 8:19).

The description of Mary's coming child identifies him definitely as the long-awaited Jewish Messiah. His name is to be Jesus, "The LORD is salvation." Like John he will be "great." The omission, however, of the expression, "before the Lord," used of John (vs. 15), sets Jesus in a special relation to God, as does the description "the Son of the Most High" (vs. 32). Jesus' position as heir of "the throne of his father David," and the eternity of his reign, clearly point him out as Messiah (II Sam. 7:12-16; Isa. 9:6-7; Ps. 132:11-12; Daniel 7:14; Hosea 3:5).

The means by which the birth of Jesus is to be accomplished is described with exquisite spiritual insight. There is no hint whatsoever of any physical act. There is no procreation, as in pagan myths, resulting from the union between a god and a woman. Jesus' birth is the creative act of the Holy Spirit pictured as the overshadowing of the power of the Most High (vs. 35). The word "overshadow" is the same word used of the cloud out of which the voice spoke at the Transfiguration (9:34). In both places it refers to the cloud in which God's glory was manifested (Exod. 40:34-38; see also Exod. 13:21; 14:19-20; 16:10; 19:9; 34:5). The cloud of God's glory made his presence visible to men, yet at the same time hid him from the eyes of men and preserved the mystery of his being. It both revealed God, and concealed him. So, the birth of Jesus is the mysterious event whereby God revealed himself in a creative act whose nature is totally hidden from us. It calls for worship, not explanations.

To encourage Mary's faith, she was given the sign that her kinswoman, Elizabeth, was also the object of God's grace in the gift of a miraculously conceived son. Furthermore, the angel made obvious reference to the gracious act of God in the gift of a son to Sarah (vs. 37; see also Gen. 18:14). This was not only to encourage Mary's faith, but to indicate that her child was to be the final fulfillment of the promise made to Abraham, that by him "all the families of the earth will be blessed" (Gen. 12:3, margin; see also Gen. 15:1-6; 17:15-21; 21:1-7). Jesus is the culmination of all that God has been doing since the days of Abraham.

Mary's response was one of full surrender, which most great paintings of the Annunciation have captured. The announcement made to her could well have had frightful social consequences.

In the Jewish custom of that day, an engagement was as binding
as a marriage. To be God's servant, Mary had to expose herself
to the misunderstanding of Joseph (Matt. 1:18-25), to the possible loss of her reputation and the curse of being considered a
sinful woman, and to possible death by stoning (Deut. 22:23-24).
She risked all this in surrender to the will of God.

Mary hastened off to visit Elizabeth as the angel had suggested.
By the inspiration of the Holy Spirit, in a moment of extreme
emotional exaltation, Elizabeth recognized in Mary the mother
of Messiah (1:39-45). If her own miraculously conceived son
was the promised forerunner (1:13-17), who else could Mary's
son be but the Messiah whose way her son was to prepare?

Mary responded in what has come to be known as the "Magnificat," which is the first word of her song in the Latin Bible.
Her words combine rejoicing over her own exalted position (vss.
47-49) with the consciousness that through her God is fulfilling
his promise to Israel (vss. 54-55). Jesus is not only her son, he
is Abraham's offspring (Gal. 3:15-16), he is "great David's
greater Son." Mary's hymn also combines God's might and his
mercy (vss. 49-50). It is built up largely out of Old Testament
materials (see particularly I Sam. 2:1-10). Its leading thought is
of the inbreaking of the Kingdom to which the whole Old Testament had been pointing. All existing order will be turned upside
down, all present standards of measurement will be reversed (vss.
51-53). This, however, is all the result of God's mercy (vss. 50,
54). But how this is to be done—through the suffering and death
of the child of promised birth—is not yet hinted. The expression
of the hope is purely Old Testament in form. These early hymns
go back very near to the original sources, and were compara-
tively untouched by later Christian theology.

Two questions plague the modern mind concerning the story
of the Virgin Birth of Jesus. What is its origin? and What is its
meaning for Christian faith? Many have seen its origin in a
combination of Old Testament prophecy and pagan legend. The
Greek translation of Isaiah 7:14 speaks of a virgin conceiving a
son. There were also pagan legends about the procreation of
children through relations between gods and women. To account
for Luke's story of the Virgin Birth on such grounds, however,
would seem to fly in the face of the facts. Even though Matthew
quotes Isaiah 7:14 in his account, Luke does not. Luke's story is
so different from Matthew's that it indicates a belief in the

Virgin Birth in the Early Church quite independent of Isaiah 7:14.

As to pagan legends, two things are clear. First, the New Testament, as the Old, rejected pagan mythology as demonic. It would hardly, then, in this crucial instance, call on pagan mythology to explain the birth of Jesus. Secondly, a comparison of the story with pagan myths makes it impossible to believe that they have the same origin. The myths are crude, sensual, revolting. Luke's story is delicate, spiritual, uplifting. Neither the ideas nor the language bear any relation to pagan stories.

It is more natural to accept Luke's story as the description of transcendent fact, like that of the Transfiguration and the Resurrection, which are facts, but go far beyond mere facts. When eternity touches time, real events take place, but they go far beyond our poor powers of understanding. Furthermore, the creation of such a myth was quite unnecessary, for no direct mention is made of the Virgin Birth in the New Testament save in the accounts of Matthew and Luke. A high view of Jesus was quite possible apart from the Virgin Birth.

Historically, Luke was far closer to the facts than we are, and we have nothing but his story to go on. There is no reason, intellectual or religious, historical or theological, why faith cannot accept Luke's story reverently and gladly as fact.

Having said that, however, the question must still be faced of its meaning for faith. At this point, much misunderstanding must be cleared away. If we accept the New Testament story, we must use it in New Testament ways. First, we must be content to put the Virgin Birth in its New Testament position in the whole structure of faith. It is not the foundation on which faith rests, but a part of its crowning glory which itself rests on the foundation. Had the Virgin Birth been a part of the foundation of the faith, it is difficult to see how the Early Church could have taken its gospel to the world for years without the slightest mention of it. Neither in the preaching of the Early Church recorded in Acts, nor in the theology set forth in Paul's letters, is anything whatsoever made of the Virgin Birth. The Church had a complete saving gospel, which Paul called "the power of God for salvation" (Rom. 1:16), without the slightest mention of the Virgin Birth.

The bedrock foundation of the faith is the resurrection of Jesus, not the manner of his birth. Paul wrote, "If Christ has not been raised, then our preaching is in vain and your faith is in vain" (I Cor. 15:14). He did not write this about the Virgin

Birth. The clearest way to see this is to look at the Gospels themselves. Mark has no story of Jesus' birth yet he tells of the Resurrection. If we had only Mark, would we have a gospel? Most
assuredly. On the other hand, Luke and Matthew both tell of the
Virgin Birth. Suppose we left the birth stories in them but elimi-
nated the Resurrection, would we have a gospel? Clearly, No.
This indicates, then, the different place the birth stories have in
the structure of faith from that of the Resurrection.

Since this is true, neither Jesus' deity nor his sinlessness rests
on the Virgin Birth. Rather, the Virgin Birth rests on them. The
first use made of the Virgin Birth in Christian history was to
prove the *humanity* of Jesus, not his deity. The earliest heresy in
the Church was that which denied Jesus' real humanity. To this
the Church replied, Jesus was a man for he was "born of woman"
(Gal. 4:4), in the womb of the Virgin Mary. Neither the New
Testament nor the Early Church ever rested Jesus' deity on his
birth. For them he was designated "Son of God in power . . . by
his resurrection from the dead" (Rom. 1:4). As to Jesus' sinlessness, no point was ever made either by the New Testament or the
Early Church that Jesus was sinless because of the method of his
birth. Jesus' sinlessness was not a theological theory, but a fact
of his human experience. Jesus was sinless simply because he did
no sin (John 8:46; Heb. 4:15; I Peter 2:22-23). To argue that
Jesus was sinless because he had no human father is unbiblical
and to be rejected. This sort of thing leads to the Roman Catholic
logic that has to make Mary sinless in order to preserve the sinlessness of Jesus by an untainted birth. The New Testament knows
of no such thing.

Another approach wholly contrary to the New Testament is to
try to prove the Virgin Birth scientifically, by what scientists call
parthenogenesis. This is the biological term describing procreation in plant and animal life without union of the sexes. The argument runs: It is now possible to prove scientifically that a child
might be born to a human mother without male fertilization.
Hence, Jesus could have been born without human father. Since
this passes under the cloak of science, and the modern mind is
conditioned to believe anything that science is supposed to have
proved, many are reassured in this way about the Virgin Birth.

Actually, such reassurance is not only far from the biblical
faith, it misses entirely the meaning of the Virgin Birth. If one
could prove scientifically, in a fashion that a panel of creditable

scientists would unanimously approve, that Jesus was actually born without human father, one would have proved nothing about the New Testament meaning of the Virgin Birth. All that such an investigation would prove is that a boy came into the world without benefit of father. The New Testament faith is that in the birth of Jesus, *God came into the world!* This is something quite beyond a biological fact. And it can neither be proved nor disproved by science. It is rather something to be believed, or disbelieved. There is no proof, only testimony. One must believe that in the Virgin Birth God entered human life redemptively, and that *he did so for me!*

What, then, is the religious meaning of the Virgin Birth in Luke's Gospel? First, it shows that Jesus' coming was *God's action*, not man's. God alone brings salvation! In a normal birth, man participates with God in his creative work. But salvation can never be wrought by the will of man. Man does not help God save him! God begins, continues, and completes the work of salvation. Man can but believe, surrender, accept, praise, serve, as did Mary. God came to earth without human choice or aid.

Again, the Virgin Birth suggests that in Jesus, God *began the creation of a new humanity*. Just as the first Adam came directly by the creative act of God, so Jesus, as the "last Adam" (I Cor. 15:45; Rom. 5:12-21; I Cor. 15:22), came directly from God as the beginning of a "new creation" (II Cor. 5:17). The chain of cause and effect was broken. Here was the creation of a new order of life, the eternal order, which could not be captive to death as the order of the old Adam was. It is this new creation to which the Virgin Birth testifies.

The Virgin Birth also attests the fact that Jesus was *born as God's Son and Messiah*, and did not become so at a later time, as for example, at the Baptism or the Resurrection. He did not achieve Sonship by good behavior. He was not accepted as God's Son as the reward for spiritual accomplishment. He was not a mere man promoted to a special relation to God. He was God's Son and Messiah from the beginning. This One born of the Virgin Mary existed with God from all eternity. His birth was a real incarnation, a real coming of God himself into human flesh.

We may sum it all up by saying that in Jesus' birth by a Virgin there is something inherently right, something wholly congruous with all that Jesus was, and is, and shall forever be. Here is abiding mystery and glorious suggestiveness which does not yield itself to argument and proof. It summons to worship and faith. The surest path to the acceptance of the mystery of his birth is to believe the mystery of his Person.

Birth of Forerunner (1:57-80)

The birth of John was a stirring event. It was a sign of God's "mercy" (vs. 58) that a child should be born to Elizabeth in her old age. How great that mercy was, however, in choosing him as the forerunner of Messiah, the people did not know. That is still the secret of the parents, save as Zechariah hints of it in his song of praise. Because of the strangeness of the events, "marvel" and "fear" and rumor ran rampant (vss. 63-66). In the light of the strong Messianic hope in the hearts of the Jews at that time, and the obvious special relation of God to this boy's birth, it is not surprising that all should wonder, "What then will this child be?" (vs. 66).

The prophetic song of Zechariah (vss. 68-79) is couched in Old Testament terms, saying nothing about John's work as a baptizer, nor his future martyrdom, nor the sufferings of Messiah whose way he was to prepare. This strongly suggests that it truly reflects what was in Zechariah's mind at that time, and has not been colored by later events.

This song, the Benedictus, named for its first word in the Latin Bible, is divided into two parts. The first (vss. 68-75) deals with the salvation now about to break in through the coming of the Messiah in the child of Mary. In accord with God's promise to the Fathers through the prophets (vss. 70, 73), he is now about to redeem his people (vs. 68). The redemption is called a "visit," a mighty intervention of God after a period of apparent inactivity, to save his people and overcome his enemies. It is also described as raising up "a horn of salvation," an Old Testament figure of strength, based on the might of the horn of a wild bull (Pss. 18:2-3; 132:17; Ezek. 29:21). Salvation is to come through a member of "the house of his servant David" (vs. 69), thus fulfilling the Messianic promise made to David.

In what would this salvation consist? As the first Exodus from Egypt released them from their enemies so that they could serve God in the way he commanded (Exod. 5:1-3; 7:16; Ps. 106: 7-12), so this would be a new Exodus, whereby they would be free of Roman demands which kept them from serving God ac-

cording to his will. There is no note of vengeance on enemies,
only freedom from them, so that "without fear, in holiness and
righteousness" (vss. 74-75), they could serve God. This suggests
that there was a spiritual nucleus in Israel who saw that salvation
must consist not only in political but also in religious deliverance.

The second part of the Benedictus centers on the mission of
John. He is "the prophet of the Most High" whose function it is
to prepare the hearts of the people to receive God's "visit." This
is to be done by proclaiming "the forgiveness of their sins,
through the tender mercy of . . . God" (vss. 76-78). Repentance
which leads to forgiveness is John's message (3:3), whereby the
people were prepared to receive Jesus. It is significant that Jesus'
first disciples were followers of John (John 1:35-51). The final
picture of the Messianic salvation is that of the rising of the sun.
God's people have been sitting in darkness, like travelers who
cannot move at night. Psalm 107:10-14 pictures their darkness
as that of manacled prisoners, sitting in the very "shadow of
death." But now the dawn comes, to light their way out of captivity and distress into God's "way of peace" (vs. 79). The Messianic Age for which Israel has hoped so long is breaking in. John
heralds the coming dawn. Jesus is the "sun" who bursts over the
horizon in splendor (see Mal. 4:2). They do not yet know that
it will be the splendor of a cross.

John dwelt apart, in the wilderness, which was a favorite
training ground for God's servants (vs. 80). Moses had his training there (Exod. 3). The whole nation spent a period of forty
years there, where they received their law and their worship
(Exodus and Deuteronomy). It was fitting that he who prepared
the people for the new Exodus should spend his days of preparation in the wilderness. It has been remarked that in God's Kingdom, the wilderness is often more important than the universities.

Birth of Messiah (2:1-21)

The story of the birth of Jesus is the most amazing "good
news" (vs. 10) ever to fall on human ears. Here is the hinge on
which history turns, the dividing point between old and new, the
single event which gives meaning to all other events. And yet,
how naturally it is told. Two verses suffice to tell all that took
place at the birth (vss. 6-7). Nothing unusual happened, save
that the child was born in a stable, had a cattle trough for his

first cradle, and his mother was probably unattended (vs. 7 implies that Mary herself wrapped him in swaddling cloths). "How silently the wondrous gift is given!" The birth of a baby, like millions of other babies, save poorer and more unnoticed than most—and God has entered human life! Would it have been told this way if it were not true?

The historical situation in which Luke sets the birth of Jesus has long been the subject for debate. Jesus lived in Nazareth, in Galilee. Why, then, was he born in Bethlehem of Judea? Some have seen Old Testament proof-texting at work here. Micah said something about Messiah's birth in Bethlehem (Micah 5:2). Therefore, it is alleged, Matthew and Luke contrived to have him born there to fulfill this prophecy. Of Luke this can hardly be said, for he makes no direct use of the Micah prophecy. Furthermore, the Jewish conceptions of the Messiah were varied, and in some of them Bethlehem played no role (John 7:27). Hence, it was not really necessary to have Jesus born in Bethlehem to believe in him as Messiah.

Former study failed to find an enrollment under Quirinius earlier than A.D. 7, although Jesus was born likely somewhere between 7 B.C. and 4 B.C. (see the discussion of 1:5-25). More recent study, however, has produced evidence tending to support Luke in his historic facts. It is known that the Romans forced owners of property to return to the place of the possession to have it recorded for tax purposes. These enrollments sometimes took years—40 years in Gaul!—for they were strongly resisted. It is quite possible that the enrollment under Quirinius was begun long before A.D. 7, and that Luke's historic facts are exact.

To be overly concerned about this, however, is to miss the point of Luke's reference. He was not at all interested in giving us the precise date of Jesus' birth. He was rather doing something much more profound. He was giving us the clue to the meaning of history. By the decree of Augustus the Messiah was born where God had chosen. In setting the Babe over against the Caesar, Luke is proclaiming that *God is Lord of history*. History is ruled not by fate, nor by the will of man, but by God. Not Caesar, but Christ, is Lord (vs. 11).

Jesus' birth is set over against the Caesar, too, because Jesus is "a Savior" (vs. 11). Augustus was called "savior." His word was called "gospel" (see the Introduction). But Augustus' "good news" would ultimately turn to bad news. His "salvation" could not meet the deepest needs of men. His kingdom could not last. Here was the true "Savior," sent from God, who should meet men at the deep level of "the forgiveness of their sins" (1:77). "Of his kingdom there will be no end" (1:33).

The birth of Messiah was not first proclaimed in Caesar's halls nor in Herod's palace, but to humble shepherds in the fields. Here began the total reversal of the values of this world, of which Mary spoke in the Magnificat. Heaven's richest treasure was given to "those of low degree" (1:51-53). "I bring *you* good news . . . for *to you* is born . . . a Savior" (2:10-11). The news was for "all the people" (vs. 10), but they would have to become as humble as these shepherds to receive it, yes, even as "a child" (18:17).

The angel's description of the newborn Babe involved three things: his function, his office, and his dignity (vs. 11). His *function* was to be "Savior," which he himself later described in the words: "For the Son of man came to seek and to save the lost" (19:10). His *office* was that of the "Christ," or Messiah. He was to be King over God's people, fulfilling all the rich promises for which Israel had been waiting through the centuries (II Sam. 7:12-16; Matt. 2:1-2). His *dignity* is seen in the word "Lord." This is the word used in both Old and New Testaments to describe God himself. Here is the One in whom God has appeared in human history to establish his Lordship over the entire universe (Phil. 2:11; Eph. 1:20-21; Col. 2:9-10, 15).

The sign given to the shepherds to confirm the "good news" of the angel was strange, but full of meaning (2:12). The cry of a baby, the smell of a stable, the age-worn trough of stone, the crunch of dry hay—not here would men have expected to find their Deliverer. Not in this fashion would men have looked for God's visit to earth. But this was the angel's sign—"a babe . . . swaddling cloths . . . a manger."

The song of the "multitude of the heavenly host" is difficult to translate (vs. 14). The difficulty is with the word "pleased." Does it refer to a disposition of men toward God which is pleasing to him? Or to a disposition of God toward men? Recently discovered parallels in the Dead Sea Scrolls indicate that the expression means "men of God's favor." Hence, there is glory to God and peace among men on earth, because it pleased God, in his grace, to send his Son into the world. The peace is not political peace, nor sentimental good will, for Jesus came not to "bring

peace, but a sword," even dividing families over loyalty to him
(Matt. 10:34-39; Luke 12:51-53). It is rather the peace of a right
relation to God, through the forgiveness of sins (Luke 1:77).

The shepherds went to investigate the sign offered by the angel, and found just what they had been told—parents, a Babe,
and a manger. They rejoiced in what they had found, and told
others of the appearance of the angels to them in the fields.
Those who heard "wondered at what the shepherds told them"
(2:18), impressed and amazed, perhaps touched with superstitious wonder, but finding nothing in the Babe to confirm the report, or to stir their hopes. Mary, on the other hand, found that
what they said accorded with what the angel had announced to
her (1:31-33). She kept her secret, pondering all in her heart,
awaiting the child's growth and manifestation (vs. 19). As a
devout member of Israel, she had the child circumcised at the end
of eight days (Jesus was born a Jew, born "under the law," Gal.
4:4; see Lev. 12:3), and gave him the name commanded by the
angel—Jesus (vs. 21). In this name she expressed her faith and
hope, for it means, "The LORD is salvation."

Dedication of Messiah (2:22-40)

Luke tells us much about the poverty of Jesus' parents in a
subtle way, by describing the offering they made—"a pair of
turtledoves, or two young pigeons" (vs. 24). If a woman could
afford it, she was to offer a lamb and a young pigeon or a turtledove. But "if she cannot afford a lamb," then a turtledove or a
young pigeon could be substituted for the lamb (Lev. 12:8). How
often this had to be resorted to we do not know, but it at least
indicates that Jesus' parents were numbered with the common
folk.

Luke's emphasis that all was done "according to the law"
(2:22, 23, 24, 39) shows how fully Jesus was identified with his
people. He was not above the Law, but under the Law, living out
a life of complete obedience to God under the conditions common to his people. His coming did not do away with God's Law.
That had to be fulfilled either by us, or by God himself *for* us.
The latter is what Jesus came to do (Matt. 5:17-20).

Luke shows the vital connection between the Old Testament
and the New by giving us the story of Simeon and Anna and their
part in the dedication of Jesus. They represent the best of the Old

Israel, "righteous and devout, looking for the consolation of Israel" (vss. 25, 37-38). Their hopes, piety, and prayers were directed toward the future, when God would bring the "consolation" and "redemption" promised by the prophets in the Messianic Age (Isa. 40:1-2). Quickened by the Holy Spirit, Simeon saw in the baby Jesus the Child of his hopes. Taking him in his arms, he broke out in praise to God in what has come to be called the "Nunc Dimittis"—the two first words in the Latin version (vss. 29-35). After blessing God for the personal gift of seeing the Messiah, he spoke prophetically of his mission. The wonder of Jesus' parents at Simeon's words lay in the fact that they went beyond those of the angel (1:32-33), in mentioning his mission to the Gentiles (vs. 32; see Isa. 42:6; 49:6). The mission was spoken of as "a light," not so much a light for pagan minds, but, in the sense already seen (1:79), the light which would guide men out of the darkness of death's shadow into the way of God's forgiveness. (See Isaiah 49:6, where light is equated with salvation.)

The most startling thing about Simeon's words is that they introduce for the first time the note of sorrow into the story of Jesus' birth (vss. 34-35). All the songs hitherto have spoken only of joy. Here is sadness. God's saving action always produces a crisis, a division, depending on men's response. All Israel looked for political deliverance. Only the Remnant sought spiritual deliverance. It was plain, therefore, that One who came to be a "revelation to the Gentiles" (vs. 32) rather than to conquer them, would be rejected. Many would "fall" over him. He would be "a sign that is spoken against" (vs. 34). The real motives hidden in the hearts of men would "be revealed," for they would have to decide either for him or against him. The outcome would be suffering which would pierce Mary's soul like a sword (vs. 35). Thus early the shadow of the Cross falls upon the story.

The prophetess, Anna, added her word to that of Simeon, speaking of Jesus "to all who were looking for the redemption of Jerusalem" (vs. 38). This group was small, and the fulfillment of their hopes lay yet more than thirty years away, in a Cross and a Resurrection. But with all the truly faithful in the Old Testament, they "died in faith, not having received what was promised, but having seen it and greeted it from afar" (Heb. 11:13).

The Temple where Jesus was dedicated was magnificent beyond words. More than half a century was required to build it.

It was projected by Herod as a memorial to himself. He determined to make it larger and more glorious than Solomon's Temple. Its dome was covered by pure gold leaf. Its altar and utensils were glittering and majestic. It was the center of all the hopes of every Jew throughout the world. It was filled with priests, busy with their official duties but dull to their spiritual function. To this Temple Jesus was brought. He drew no attention from the officials. Only a few pious folk had their hopes stirred by his presence. Here is the Old Israel in all its outward, official splendor, set over against the New Israel embodied in this Babe. The simple goodness of this Child will ultimately be pitted against all the might of official Judaism. One day he will enter this very Temple in wrath and brand it "a den of robbers" (Luke 19:46). His spiritual authority will be challenged by the official authority of the chief priests and scribes and elders (20:2). One can already feel that the Baby and the Temple cannot well exist together. The first faint echoes of Jesus' later words can almost be heard: "There shall not be left here one stone upon another that will not be thrown down" (21:6).

The infancy story comes to its close with one of Luke's favorite short summaries, which connects with the story to follow. The lad grew in body, mind, and spirit. All is natural and normal. Here is real "incarnation." God actually became *man*, taking upon himself all the limitations, weaknesses, necessities of growth, which are the lot of man—all save sin (Heb. 2:17; 4:15).

THE NATURE OF JESUS' MESSIAHSHIP: THE SUFFERING SERVANT
Luke 2:41—4:30

The first impression which this section makes is one of disunity. The stories which make it up seem to be unrelated in *content*. The experience of a spiritually precocious lad (2:41-52); the dramatic appearance of a fiery reformer (3:1-22); a family tree (3:23-38); an inner struggle of the Gospel's central figure (4:1-13); the sermon of a famous man in his home town synagogue (4:16-30)—what connection have these? The same impression of disjointedness is felt in the references to *time*. Twelve years have elapsed between the birth stories and the first event (2:42). Eighteen years elapse between the first incident and the second (3:23). The family tree is chronologically out of place. The whole time scheme seems marked by disarray. An examination of Luke's use of *sources* adds to the impression of disjointedness. Some of his material he takes from Mark, some from Q, and some from his own special source (see the Introduction). Everywhere the surface impression is one of bungling disunity, like an unrelated assembly of snapshots stuck together in a scrapbook without plan or artistry.

Ofttimes, however, a profound unity lies hidden beneath a superficial disunity. The words on which the story of the boy Jesus in the Temple turns are "my *Father's* house" (2:49). The climax of John's ministry is the baptism of Jesus, where a voice from heaven says, "my beloved *Son*" (3:22). "The *son* of" is the characteristic phrase of the family tree (3:23-38). Twice the expression, "If you are the *Son* of God," gives the clue to the meaning of the Temptation (4:3, 9). In the story about preaching in the Nazareth synagogue, the people at first can hardly believe their ears, and ask: "Is not this Joseph's *son?*" (4:22). Unquestionably, the element which binds all these stories into a unity is that of *sonship.* Since in four instances Jesus' sonship to God is expressed or implied (2:49; 3:22; 3:38; 4:3, 9), and in the fifth he claims to be God's "anointed" who will bring in the Messianic Age (4:18-21), the central unity of this section is clear: *Jesus is the Son of God.* Jesus is the Messianic King spoken of in the Old Testament as God's Son (II Sam. 7:14; Ps. 2:7; see also Luke 22:70; John 1:49).

Added to this is the thought that the way to become a true member of the family of God lies in him and his work. The Jews claimed to be children of God because Abraham was their "father." John insisted that this claim had no validity (Luke 3:8-9). Repentance (3:8) and faith in the "good news" of the coming Kingdom which God's Son was to bring (3:18) formed the only pathway to a right relationship to God. Tracing Jesus' genealogy all the way back to Adam suggests, too, that all men are related to what he had come to do (3:23-38). This entire section, then, states the central conviction to which Luke is seeking to lead his readers: *Jesus is the Son of God, the Messianic King who has inaugurated the Kingdom of God, and membership in this Kingdom for all other men lies in him.* Thus, Luke's "orderly account" (1:3) places after the introduction to the Gospel (1:5—2:40) a clear statement of its theme (2:41—4:30).

/o - 1 3

The Boy Jesus in the Temple:
Jesus' First Recognition of Sonship (2:41-52)

The Law prescribed that every male Jew should go up to Jerusalem for three annual Feasts: Passover, Pentecost, and Tab-
ernacles (Exod. 23:14-17; Deut. 16:16). Women did not have
to go, but often did (I Sam. 1:3-28). It was Mary's custom to go
annually (vs. 41). The Law does not specify the age when a boy
comes under its obligations. Jewish custom, however, set it at
thirteen, when a boy became a "son of the commandment."
Some parents, in order to prepare their children for this day, so
that it would not be too sudden an entrance upon adult religious
obligations, took their children to the feasts at Jerusalem before
they were thirteen. Jesus' presence at the Feast at the age of
twelve may indicate such a practice on the part of his parents.

It is not surprising that Jesus' parents did not miss him on the
homeward journey until nightfall (vss. 43-45). For protection
against robbers, it was customary for pilgrims to the Feasts to
travel in caravans. The crowds were tremendous. About 100,000
pilgrims crowded into a city of only 50,000 inhabitants. In each
caravan, family groups were often separated. Mary could well
have thought that Jesus was with Joseph, while Joseph thought
him to be with Mary, or both may have thought that he was with
relatives or friends.

"After three days" (vs. 46) probably includes the day's journey
away from Jerusalem, the journey back, and the day they found
him. He was in the Temple, taking part in the instruction of the
rabbis. Note that Luke does not say that Jesus was instructing.
He was learning. He was "listening" to them, "asking" information from them, and "answering" their questions (vss. 46-47).
They were "amazed at his understanding and his answers," for
he had a grasp of spiritual truth quite unusual for a lad of his
years. But there is no hint of anything like the boast of Josephus,
a Jewish historian of the first century A.D., who claimed to have
been questioned on points of the Law at the age of fourteen by
the High Priest and elders. Nor is there any hint of what is
found in one of the Gospels the Church rejected, which pictured
Jesus as instructing the rabbis in the Law and in prophetic mysteries, and enlightening them on astronomy, medicine, and other
learned matters. Luke's story is natural, restrained, unembellished.

It is quite natural that Mary should speak a word of gentle

rebuke, in which she reveals their "anxiety" over him (vs. 48; see also Luke 16:25, where the same word is translated "anguish"). The meaning of the whole story lies in Jesus' reply to his mother's rebuke. Mary said, "your father and I." Jesus replied, "*my* Father" (vs. 49). It is this play on the twofold filial relationship of Jesus—to his parents and to God—which leads to the heart of the story.

Jesus was conscious of a unique relationship to God. Why should he not be in the Temple? It was God's house, and there he was at home. This was not a studied answer. It was rather the spontaneous expression of a deep inner consciousness. He was subject to his earthly parents (vs. 51), yet at the same time he was conscious of a higher relationship more intimate and more meaningful. The Old Testament had called God "Father" (Deut. 32:6; Isa. 63:16; Ps. 103:13). The term, however, either referred to God as Father of the nation or was used as an illustration—"*as* a father." Here Jesus goes beyond these. His sense of being in his Father's house is not merely that of an Israelite, conscious that the Temple was the place where God manifested his presence. The expression on Jesus' lips is wholly personal—"*my* Father's house." In these first recorded words from Jesus' lips is seen his early *recognition* of his unique Sonship to God. Here is the first faint ray of light on his Person, which will dawn upon Jesus in all its fullness at his Baptism, and will burst on the disciples in splendor after the Resurrection.

Luke, however, carefully guards against reading too much into Jesus' consciousness at this time. Jesus is not yet fully aware of his Messiahship, nor of the full meaning of his unique relation to God. He goes home to do what a twelve-year-old should do, obey his parents (vs. 51). As a normal child, he must still develop to maturity by learning (Heb. 5:8). Hence, Luke tells us that he "increased in wisdom"—both mental and moral insight; "in stature"—physical growth; "and in favor with God and man" —spiritual excellence (vs. 52; see I Sam. 2:26). His consciousness of divine Sonship was real, but undeveloped—"faint like an echo in a dream." He was not a God who merely looked like a child, in whom growth would have been impossible. He was truly human in body, mind, and spirit, living under all the limitations common to man—save sin.

Mary's inability to "understand" (vs. 50) what he said was the first light stroke of the "sword" which was to pierce her heart

(2:35). As mother of Messiah, she had a son, and yet, in a sense, she did not. He did not belong to her, but to all men, in a way that Mary could not at that time understand (see Luke 8:19-21; 11:27-28). There is wisdom, however, in Mary's dealing with her lack of understanding. When God's truth is not clear, do not cast it off; hide it in the heart and wait for fuller light (vs. 51).

The Baptism of Jesus:
God's Vindication of Jesus' Sonship (3:1-22)

It is difficult to imagine what the rise of John the Baptist meant to his people. It was "more important far than war or revolution." The characteristic way that God had made known his will in Israel in the past was through prophets. But prophecy had been silent for more than four centuries. The belief was widespread, however, that when the Messianic Age came, prophecy would reappear (Joel 2:28; Mal. 3:1; 4:5). When, therefore, John the Baptist made his sudden and dramatic appearance in the Judean wilderness, it was like a bolt out of the blue. Here was the prophet who was to prepare the way for God's decisive action! Here was the signal for the coming of the New Age! Now was the hour of God's deliverance of a people frustrated by centuries of delay! The End Time had come!

Luke makes this clear in two ways. First, he describes John's prophetic role in the exact words of the calls of the earlier prophets—"the word of God came to John" (vs. 2; see I Sam. 15:10; II Sam. 7:4; I Kings 17:2; Jer. 2:1). Prophecy had again arisen! Second, he takes great pains to set John's appearance in its historical framework. He mentions not only the political rulers at that time (vs. 1), but also the religious leaders of Judaism (vs. 2). He means by this to suggest that Judaism had reached its climax in John; the end toward which it was moving was announced by him. But more than that, the end toward which *all* history had been moving was about to take place—the coming of the Kingdom of God. "All flesh shall see the salvation of God" (vs. 6). In that which John announced, both secular history and religious history would reach their fulfillment.

If, however, God's decisive hour in history was about to break in, this called for an equally decisive response on the part of man. When oriental kings made journeys into remote parts of their realms, heralds were sent ahead to announce their coming.

Roads had to be made where there were none—valleys had to be filled, and hills made low. And where there were roads, they had to be straightened and smoothed (vss. 4-5). John is the herald. His message was: The King is coming! Prepare the way! How was this to be done? By repentance, by a radical change of heart which would manifest itself in works that gave evidence of it.

The thoroughgoing nature of John's message is seen in his demand that everyone repent—and give witness to repentance by baptism. Many of the Jews expected judgment to fall on the Gentiles when the Kingdom came. They, however, as children of Abraham, would escape judgment and be heirs of the Kingdom (vs. 8). John reversed all this. In effect, he excommunicated the whole nation. It was not sufficient to be a descendant of Abraham. God had no more regard for their pride of birth than for desert stones. God's judgment was about to fall. Those who did not "bear fruits that befit repentance" would be destroyed (vss. 8-9). Only those who repented, acknowledging that they were sinners before God and desiring the gift of a new life, could withstand the judgment when it came. Only they would receive the forgiveness which the Messiah would bring.

This break with current Judaism was dramatized by the fact that John appeared not in Jerusalem, the "holy" city, where official Judaism centered, but in the wilds of the Judean wilderness. Repentance meant a break with what Jerusalem stood for at that time, and an acknowledgment that it was under the judgment of God. The demand of John was that men do this immediately and decisively. The rite of baptism dramatized all this. One was born a child of Abraham, the sign of which was circumcision. He must now, by his own decision, confess that Abraham's children had failed. He must acknowledge that his only hope for entrance into the coming Kingdom was God's merciful forgiveness and cleansing from sin.

Baptism, however, was not a magical rite which imparted blessing in itself. When the multitudes flocked to John to be baptized, he insisted that the rite was of no value save as it testified to a deep inner change of heart (vss. 7-9). This change of heart, however, was not some dramatic act, far removed from the common round of life. It was to be manifested by living in hope of the coming Kingdom in the ordinary tasks of every day. Those who had an excess of clothing and food were to share it with those who had none (vs. 11). Tax collectors, excluded from the

Kingdom by the rabbis because they were in the employ of the Romans and were considered traitors to their own people, were not to leave their jobs but to discharge them with integrity and scrupulous honesty (vss. 12-13). Soldiers were to serve faithfully, content with their pay, and not to enrich themseves falsely either by violence or by fraud (vs. 14). This counsel of John is not to be thought of as mere moralizing, nor as salvation by works. Had he stood for this, he would not have broken with the religious leaders of his day. He is not saying that if men are generous, honest, and faithful, they will thereby earn the right to be members of the coming Kingdom. He is rather saying that if one acknowledges his unworthiness and accepts God's gracious gift of entrance into the coming Kingdom, he will show it by ethical behavior toward his fellow man. This is not the ethics of legalism, but the ethics of gratitude. It is the extension in grateful service of the hand of one who has first beat upon his breast crying, "God, be merciful to me a sinner!" (18:13).

The appearance of John created such a stir in Judea, and so fanned into flame the Messianic hopes of the people, that many began to wonder whether he might be the Messiah (vs. 15). This John denied in the strongest terms. There was a "mightier" One coming, so much greater than he that he was not worthy even to offer him the menial service of untying his sandals. He would actually bring what John's baptism with water signified—the gift of the Holy Spirit, which was the sign of entrance into the Messianic Age (vs. 16). The "fire" connected with the baptism of the Holy Spirit likely refers to the purifying of the Spirit's work. In a passage in Malachi which seems to lie behind Luke's whole description of the work of John, the "messenger" sent to prepare the way of the Lord is to be "like a refiner's fire." He is to "purify" and "refine" the people so that they may "present right offerings to the LORD" (Mal. 3:1-3). Water cleanses the outside alone. Fire penetrates to the deepest recesses and purifies the inner life. But those who do not repent will be destroyed (vs. 17). The coming Kingdom will bring a great separation.

But just as prophets of old had to suffer for the word which they spoke, so this one who gathered up the whole of Old Testament prophecy and pointed it directly toward Jesus, likewise had to suffer. Luke ends his story of John by telling of his imprisonment under Herod, whose evil life he had rebuked (vss. 19-20). In his suffering, without knowing it, John was a forerunner of him who came to be the Suffering Servant (see Matthew 17:12, where Jesus connects John's sufferings with his own).

Since Luke conceives of John's work purely in relation to that of Jesus, the most significant fact of his career was his baptism of Jesus. No description is given of the Baptism itself. The emphasis is placed rather on what happened to Jesus in that moment. The record is brief, but of extreme importance.

The heart of the story is the voice from heaven (vs. 22). It probably was heard by Jesus only, for it was addressed directly to him—"Thou." The exact form of this experience is a mystery. Luke is interested not in psychological explanations of the inner life of Jesus, but rather in the theological meaning of the experience. It is significant, however, that the voice spoke words of Scripture. What happened came out of Jesus' contemplation of his mission in the light of the Old Testament. Luke adds that it was in answer to his prayer. The root of the experience, then, was prayerful study of the Scriptures to determine God's will for his life. This is of paramount importance, for it suggests that if Jesus came to clarity about himself and his mission by the Holy Spirit's illumination of the Scriptures, we are not likely to find a better way for ourselves. The Holy Spirit speaks through the Scriptures, not apart from them.

The voice echoes two Old Testament passages. The first half of the declaration comes from Psalm 2:7—"You are my son." The second half comes from Isaiah 42:1—"in whom my soul delights." This suggests that two strands of Old Testament thought which seem for the most part to have developed independently were brought firmly together in the mind of Jesus. Psalm 2 pictured one who bore a special relation to God as Son, "anointed" or commissioned to carry out his purposes (Ps. 2:2). The mission given to him was to subdue the nations and bring the ends of the earth into subjection to God's Lordship (Ps. 2:8). But what was the method whereby this was to be done? Clearly that of coercive force. "You shall break them with a rod of iron, and dash them in pieces like a potter's vessel" (Ps. 2:9).

Isaiah 42 is both similar and dissimilar to this. Instead of a Son, the chosen of God is a Servant. In this lies no contradiction, for what is true sonship but obedient service to the will of a father? The mission of the Servant is identical with that of the Son—"he will bring forth justice to the nations" (Isa. 42:1). His task is to bring all peoples under the divine sovereignty. But what

of the method by which this was to be done? At this point there
is a radical difference from the Second Psalm. Instead of violently smashing all opposition before him, "He will not cry or
lift up his voice, or make it heard in the street" (Isa. 42:2). He
is so gentle that he will not break off an already bent reed, nor
snuff out the wick that gives no light (Isa. 42:3). He will un-
dertake his task by a method which seems doomed to failure
from the very start, a method which will tempt him to be "dis-
couraged." Yet he will "not fail . . . till he has established justice
in the earth" (Isa. 42:4). The full meaning of this discouraging
method is set forth in Isaiah 53. It is the method of suffering
love, which destroys the opposition to God's sovereign rule in
the earth not by violent assertion but by redemptive suffering.

The Son and the Servant are one and the same! This, Jesus
had found in the Old Testament. The heavenly voice now confirms his conviction and seals it with the gift of the Holy Spirit.
The early surmise of the twelve-year-old boy has grown through
the years, tested by life and enriched by the Holy Scriptures. To
the One who eighteen years before had said, "my *Father*" (2:49),
the vindicating voice from heaven says, "my *Son*" (3:22). But
true sonship means obedient service. The Son must fulfill the role
of the Servant.

This gives us the clue to the meaning of Jesus' baptism. John's
baptism was "a baptism of repentance for the forgiveness of
sins" (3:3). Was Jesus baptized for his own sins? Certainly not,
according to the New Testament writers (see II Cor. 5:21; Heb.
4:15; 7:26; I Peter 2:22; I John 3:5). Rather he was baptized
for the sins of others. Isaiah 53 makes this clear. There the Servant is pictured as one whose wounds and bruises were for the
"iniquities" of others (vss. 5-6). He was "stricken for the trans-
gression of my people" (vs. 8). He was made "an offering for
sin" (vs. 10). "He bore the sin of many" by "pour[ing] out his
soul to death" (vs. 12). Thus Luke couples Jesus' baptism with
that of the people—"when all the people were baptized, and
when Jesus also had been baptized" (3:21). In his first public
act, the Servant identified himself with the sins of his people, and
was baptized for their sake, not his own. He took upon himself
all the sins which all the people brought to the Jordan.

It is plain, therefore, that right from the beginning of Jesus'
public ministry, he was headed for the Cross. How clear the details of the outcome of his choice were at that moment we can-

not know. We do know, however, that *in principle* he accepted the role of the Servant who "humbled himself and became obedient unto death, even death on a cross" (Phil. 2:8). The Suffering Servant is the key which unlocks the meaning of the entire New Testament, yes, even of the whole Bible (see Luke 24:25-27, 44-47; Acts 2:22-33; 3:13, 18, 26; 4:27, 30; 8:32-35; Phil. 2:5-11; Heb. 5:7-9; I Peter 1:11; 4:1; 5:1; Rev. 5:6, 9-12).

In addition to telling of the voice heard by Jesus at the Baptism, Luke tells us that "the heaven was opened" (vs. 21). This means that the world above sense became visible to Jesus (see Acts 7:56). The veil which divides the human and the Divine was drawn back, and Jesus entered upon a fuller fellowship with his Father than he had heretofore known. He, at this moment, knew the perfect filial relationship wherein the Father made himself and his purposes fully known, and he entered into these purposes with complete understanding and acceptance. The filial relationship of the twelve-year-old, perfect at that stage but necessarily limited, has now become complete.

This is confirmed by the gift of the Holy Spirit (vs. 22). Why the figure of the dove is used is not clear. Several guesses have been made, but it is perhaps better to confess ignorance. Luke's expression "in bodily form" is mysterious, but is intended to stress the objective reality of the experience. He does not say that the Spirit came in a "body," but "in bodily form." Nor does he say that an actual dove was present. He says "as a dove." Mark, Matthew, and John all use similar expressions (Matt. 3:16; Mark 1:10; John 1:32). Here is mystery which we do not understand, but for which a rational explanation is not important.

The important thing is that the Holy Spirit came on Jesus in a way different from what he had known before. Again we move in the twilight of mystery. We are in the near neighborhood of the Trinity, where the relations between Father, Son, and Holy Spirit elude our grasp. At the Baptism, where Jesus assumes the role of the Servant and receives power to enter upon his ministry, there is an activity of the entire Godhead which bespeaks the tremendous importance of the occasion. The Father speaks and the Holy Spirit descends. The recipient of the Father's voice and of the Holy Spirit is the Son. Henceforth, there is a union between them which, rather than denying the reality of their past relations, deepens and seals them.

Jesus was not without the Holy Spirit before his baptism. He was born of the Spirit (1:35). But now, the Holy Spirit has come on him in his fullness in such a complete union that the two are inseparable in God's action and in Christian experience. (See II Corinthians 3:17, where Paul says "the Lord is the Spirit"; see also Acts 16:6-7, where "the Holy Spirit" and "the Spirit of Jesus" seem to be used interchangeably. This does not mean that they are identical, but that they are so closely related that to have one is to have both.) On others, the Holy Spirit had come in partial measure and for special periods (see I Sam. 10:6; 16: 14). But here is a coming of the Holy Spirit in a way which has no parallel in the Old Testament. On Jesus, the Spirit came in fullness and came to remain forever. For this reason, it was possible for Jesus to fulfill the mission of which John spoke, "He will baptize you with the Holy Spirit" (3:16).

The Fourth Gospel makes unmistakably plain what is implicit here in Luke, when John the Baptist says: "He on whom you see the Spirit descend and *remain,* this is he who baptizes with the Holy Spirit" (John 1:33; see also John 3:34). Jesus can now impart the Holy Spirit by imparting himself.

With this unique empowering, Jesus goes forth to the ministry of the Suffering Servant in obedience to his Father's will. What Israel had failed to do—to be God's obedient servant—Jesus now will do for them, and for all men. Here is both the New Israel and the New Adam. He must bear the sins of the many, in order that he may "make many to be accounted righteous" (Isa. 53:11; see also Rom. 5:19). This is the meaning of his baptism.

The Genealogy:
The Universal Meaning of Jesus' Sonship (3:23-38)

The genealogy of Luke faces us with difficulties, especially in the light of that of Matthew (Matt. 1:1-17). The list of names is somewhat different. Several ingenious attempts have been made to solve this problem, but none of them has more than conjectural value. The wisdom of John Wesley on this point could well be followed. He remarked that if there were any discrepancies in the two lists, it merely meant that there were errors in the public documents from which they were taken, and that the Holy Spirit did not see fit to inspire the Gospel writers to correct the court records of their day! Paul would have agreed, since he counseled Timothy to avoid "endless genealogies which promote speculations rather than the divine training that is in faith" (I Tim. 1:4; see also Titus 3:9). However difficult the genealogies of Matthew and Luke may be to harmonize, they both achieve the ends for which they are introduced. Furthermore, in Luke's case, he traces the line clear back to Adam, where he legitimately arrives, whatever be the course by which he gets there! The fact that the genealogies were traced through Joseph, though he was not the physical parent of Jesus, was no problem to Luke or to his readers. In the Orient, parenthood is not merely a matter of birth. It can be acquired. Adoptive parents are *real* parents. So can God be our Father; we have all received "adoption as sons" (Gal. 4:5).

What was the purpose of including a genealogy at all? Matthew traces the line of descent from Abraham to Jesus, showing thereby that Jesus was the true heir of Israel who gathered into himself the threads of the holy history of the people of God. But the narrow stream of holy history, made up of the story of the people of God from Abraham to Jesus, had a decisive meaning for *all* history. Although its limits were quite definite, its function, like that of the Gulf Stream, was to transform the climate of the whole ocean. Consequently, Luke traces his genealogy in the opposite direction from Matthew, beginning with Jesus, and carrying it back to "Adam" (3:38). Jesus is the climax not only of holy history but of *all* history. He not only fulfills the hopes of Israel, he brings fullness of life to *all* men. In his life, death, and resurrection, the center of all history is reached. Every life ever born, before or since, is related to him. He is the goal toward which all history moves, the end for which all things were created.

In this way, Luke was suggesting Paul's conception of Jesus as the "last Adam" (I Cor. 15:20-22, 45-49; Rom. 5:12-19). The first Adam was the originator of the old humanity, characterized by disobedience and death (Gen. 3). Here is a new Adam, the originator of a new order of humanity, characterized by obedience and eternal life. In him, estranged humanity is once more given the "power to become children of God" (John 1:12). This new Adam will perform an "act of righteousness" which will lead "to acquittal and life for all men" (Rom. 5:18). This is the significance of Luke's genealogy. It establishes the *universality* of the saving work of the Son who is the Suffering Servant.

The Temptation of Jesus:
The Son Remains the Servant (4:1-13)

The temptation of Jesus is not so much a preparation for his ministry as its opening act. He had come to be a Savior (2:11). This meant doing battle with God's enemy, whom Jesus later called "the ruler of this world" (John 12:31; 14:30; 16:11), and whom Paul termed "the god of this world" and "the prince of the power of the air" (II Cor. 4:4; Eph. 2:2). This was the first engagement with the Devil in a battle which continued to the end. It introduces us to a struggle in which no quarter may be given and no compromise is possible. It is a battle for the Lordship of the world. Either Jesus or the Devil must win, and the power of the other be broken.

Many have questioned the existence of a personal Devil and look upon him as merely a symbol of the total sin of the human race. No proof for or against such a view may be given. It is plain that Jesus believed in the reality of the Devil. One may, if he likes, discard this as a part of the time-conditioned framework of Jesus' message. May it not be, however, that Jesus plumbed the dimensions of evil at a level deeper than is possible to us? In spite of the good will and best efforts of responsible leaders, and the almost universal longing for peace on the part of the masses of all lands, human society precariously balances on the verge of self-destruction. It may well be the height of naiveté to account for this either by mere human stupidity and perverseness or the evil designs of a few wicked leaders. Belief in the existence of the Devil may solve more problems than it raises!

The nature of the Temptation experience cannot be fully understood. It was a private affair which, obviously, no one else could share. It was not the sort of thing which the Church would have created if it were not real. Hence, the story must have come from Jesus himself. What form it took to his consciousness we cannot know. It is hardly likely, however, that the Devil appeared in all his ugliness. He more likely appeared as an "angel of light" (II Cor. 11:14), using Scripture as his weapon against Jesus. Furthermore, there is no physical location from which "all the kingdoms of the world" may be seen in a moment of time (vs. 5). The story intends to make the Devil objective in the sense that he came to Jesus from without, and was not merely the reflection of the working of his own heart. Yet it is quite unlikely

that if one had been there, he could have come away with a
photograph of the Devil or a tape recording of the conversation.

A point of significance is the place which Scripture plays in
the whole encounter. In two of the temptations, the Devil tries
to mislead Jesus by a wrong use of Scripture. In all three of
them, Jesus' sword of victory is the Word of God. This testifies
to Jesus' true humanity, to his precise knowledge of the Scriptures, and to the supreme value he placed on them.

To understand the temptation of Jesus, it is necessary to relate
it directly to his baptism. Although Luke places the genealogy
between the two, he does not mean to separate them. Both Matthew and Mark likewise connect these two experiences, Mark
using the word "immediately" (Matt. 4:1; Mark 1:12). They are
two parts of one experience. They both have to do with his *mission* and the means by which it is to be achieved. The Baptism
clarified his mission as Suffering Servant. The Temptation confronted him with the costliness of this mission and tested whether
he would be obedient to it. The Temptation, therefore, was not
designed to make him doubt his Messiahship. It was rather Satan's
effort to divert him from being a *suffering* Messiah. Would he
seek to achieve his mission by fulfilling the Messianic hopes of his
people, or would he be obedient to the Father's will and go to the
Cross—a choice which meant rejection by his people right from
the start? This was what Jesus faced at the Temptation.

To this testing he was "led by the Spirit" (4:1). To face it
was his first step of obedience to his Father's will. The forty days
in the "wilderness" recall the experience of the founder of the
Old Covenant, Moses, who remained on the mountain forty days
and nights, and did not eat or drink (Deut. 9:9), and who had to
return to a rebellious people who had rejected his leadership and
his God (Deut. 9:12). It also relates to the testing of the Old
Israel in the wilderness for forty years (Deut. 8:2). They failed
in their obedience to God. Jesus, as the founder of the New
Israel, would make good where they had failed.

The first temptation was an effort to divert him from his
chosen path of suffering into becoming a "bread king," an *economic* Messiah (vs. 3). He who holds men's bread in his hands
can rule. And since Jesus was the Son of God ("since" is a better
translation than "if"), he could utilize his power to make bread
out of desert stones. By thus meeting the needs of his people, he
could win their allegiance, and ultimately conquer the whole

world. The force of this temptation lay in the fact that there
seemed to be scriptural warrant for it. Had not Moses, the leader
of the first Exodus, fed the people with manna from heaven?
(Exod. 16:4-36). If Jesus were to fulfill in a new and greater
Exodus what was begun there, why should he not follow a similar
method? (see John 6:30-31). Then, too, Jesus' own hunger at this
time made men's need for bread vivid. Since men must have
bread, why not give it to them?

Jesus' victory over this temptation came through a word of
God in the Old Testament: "Man shall not live by bread alone"
(vs. 4; Deut. 8:3). The brief record here does not complete the
verse, but Matthew indicates that the whole of it was in the mind
of Jesus: man lives "by every word that proceeds from the mouth
of God" (Matt. 4:4). Man does need bread, and need it desper-
ately. Ask some half-starved victim of a concentration camp!
But bread is not the only nor the deepest need. Fellowship with
God, growing out of obedience—even if it should mean hunger
—is man's deepest need. Jesus, therefore, refused to be diverted
from the pathway of suffering by meeting man's superficial needs
in place of his deepest needs. He also refused to use his power to
minister to his own needs. By his answer two things are plain:
he lives as man, and he lives in perfect obedience to his Father's
will. Whatever the cost of these two decisions, he will pay it.

The second temptation was to avoid suffering by using earthly
power, by becoming a *political* Messiah (vss. 5-7). Matthew,
who places this temptation last, probably gives the climactic
order, for in the light of the Jewish hopes of Jesus' day, this
temptation was probably the strongest. That is why Jesus replied
to it so decisively, "Begone, Satan!", and spoke so harshly to
Peter when he voiced the same temptation later at Caesarea
Philippi (Matt. 4:10; 16:23). Jesus grew up under Roman sovereignty. His hands labored to earn sufficient to pay Roman
taxes. He had seen the havoc wrought by Rome on his nation.
He loved his land and his people, and must have longed with
them for the day of freedom from Roman power. So the cry of
his people for political deliverance was very real and very ap-
pealing to him. One of the prayers which Jews prayed in Jesus'
day was that God would send the promised King, the Son of
David, girded with power "to annihilate the godless rulers and
to cleanse Jerusalem from the heathen," by "breaking them in
pieces with iron rods." Then "the heathen would be put under

his yoke," and "foreigners would have no right to dwell" among
the people of God. There were many Zealots who had taken up
arms against their Roman conquerors to aid God in answering
this prayer. Some even went so far as to kill their own people who
collaborated with the Romans. This is what the Jewish people desired in their Deliverer. Jesus knew this. So did the Devil!

Hence, the Evil One placed before Jesus' mind "all the kingdoms of the world in a moment of time," with all their "authority and their glory" (vss. 5-6). "To you I will give all this," he
said, if you will only "worship" me (vs. 7). Such worship would
have been an acknowledgment that the Devil owned "all this" by
right. In this way, the Tempter sought a compromise by which
he could avoid a battle to the death. It was an offer to grant Jesus
Lordship over this world, if only he would not contest the Devil's
lordship elsewhere in the universe. Not only human history, but
the world that is above history, is temporarily under the dominion
of Satan. He is at work in "the principalities and powers" of the
invisible world as well (Col. 1:16; 2:15). When the Tempter saw
One coming who was to contest his total lordship, he attempted to
escape by offering Jesus a partial Lordship which would shrink
his own dominions but not totally terminate his reign.

His claim that the earth had "been delivered" to him was partially true. He is "the ruler of this world" (John 12:31), "the
prince of the power of the air" (Eph. 2:2). But the claim, "I
give it to whom I will," was false. For his lordship is limited both
in power and duration. He was "a strong man, fully armed,"
who "guards his own palace" and whose "goods" were in peace
(Luke 11:21). But "one stronger than he" had come to "assail
him and overcome him" (Luke 11:22). His power was great,
but there was a greater power, and Satan's days were numbered.
So, with half-truth and half-falsehood, and using the Messianic
hopes of Jesus' own people whom he had come to save, Satan
assaulted the integrity of Jesus in the hope of saving himself and
his "dominion of darkness" (Col. 1:13).

Again Jesus' answer was taken from Scripture: "You shall
worship the Lord your God, and him only shall you serve" (vs.
8; Deut. 6:13). To have acknowledged Satan's lordship anywhere
in the universe, would have been a denial of the total Lordship of
God. Satan's authority was a usurped authority. It was the result
of rebellion against God, the only rightful Lord of the whole universe. The rebellion must be put down. God must reign. Jesus

must destroy "every rule and every authority and power" set against God (I Cor. 15:24). Hence, he refused Satan's offer, refused to escape suffering in order to win a partial victory, and maintained his decision to be the Servant who should obey God at any cost ("him only shall you *serve*").

Furthermore, had Jesus yielded to this temptation, he would not even have gained the true Lordship of this world. To rule by the "authority" and "glory" of this world would not have established the Kingdom of God even here on the earth. No rule based on external authority ever truly wins the allegiance of men, nor can it last. History is the graveyard of such authority. God wants the will of man, his heart, his free obedience in love. When these are given, then, and then only, is his Kingdom at work. In Jesus' own land, a good century and a half before he was born, the Maccabees had arisen in the name of religion to deliver their people by force. A truly remarkable temporary success followed. But within a brief span, the movement had lost its soul, and worse evils followed in its wake than those from which it had brought deliverance. In our own time revolutions against tyranny have soon ended in worse forms of tyranny. Coercive power may be necessary to restrain evil. But it can never bring the Kingdom of God. "The weapons of our warfare are not worldly" (II Cor. 10:4). Much as Jesus must have wished political deliverance for his people, he saw that their real needs lay deeper. They, and the whole universe, needed deliverance from Satan. Through the power of suffering love, he would "put all his enemies under his feet" (I Cor. 15:25).

The third temptation was to be a *miracle-working* Messiah, one who would win the allegiance of men by wonders (vss. 9-11). Human nature is addicted to wonders. Even in the modern world, which is heir to the Renaissance of the 15th and 16th centuries, the Enlightenment of the 18th century, and the scientific discoveries of the 19th and 20th centuries, the love of the marvelous still lingers. There is no place in the world, no matter how sophisticated, where one who performs wonders will not have a large following. This was doubly true in Jesus' day. Paul, who knew Judaism from within, said that the "Jews demand signs" (I Cor. 1:22). All through Jesus' ministry his people "sought from him a sign from heaven" (Luke 11:16, 29-32; Matt. 12:38; 16:1; Mark 8:11; John 2:18; 6:30). In the light of this, the temptation to use his power to cast himself down from the pinnacle of the Temple without injury, was both real and strong.

But why do this at the Temple? Because that was the place where the Jews were looking for a sign. For more than five centuries their hopes had been so frustrated that they felt deliverance could come only by an act of God. They, however, still had their Temple, the place of God's presence with them. It was the one visible symbol of their status as God's favored people. It therefore had become more and more the center of all their emotional ties to their history and of their hopes for the future. And had not Malachi written that "the Lord whom you seek will suddenly come to his temple"? (Mal. 3:1). What better way could there be to declare Messiahship than to make a dramatic arrival at the Temple in such fashion that the coming itself was a miracle? There was seeming justification in Scripture for such a gesture. God had promised angels to bear one up (4:10-11; Ps. 91: 11-12). Was this not the time to put God to the test? And would not such a risk of faith justify his people in believing in him?

The answer to this, too, lay in Scripture. "You shall not tempt the Lord your God" (4:12; Deut. 6:16). God's promises are not given to be used for selfish ends. Neither are they designed to surround us with the divine protection when we choose the dangers to which we shall expose ourselves. The context of the Psalm which Satan quoted makes this clear. "Because he *cleaves to me in love,* I will deliver him; I will protect him, because he *knows my name"* (Ps. 91:14). In the obedient service which flows from loving fellowship with him are God's promises validated. The path of Jesus was the path of the Servant. The protecting care of God would have to be given by the choice of his Father rather than his own desire, and in whatever measure God determined. Even the Servant would have to know an hour when it seemed that God's promises had failed. He would have to cry out, "My God, my God, why hast thou forsaken me?" (Mark 15:34). It was then that God's promise to bear him up was fulfilled at a deeper level. Through the Resurrection, God "highly exalted him and bestowed on him the name which is above every name" (Phil. 2:9). But this could come only through the humble obedience of the Servant "unto death, even death on a cross" (Phil. 2:8).

Luke's closing statement, "when the devil had ended *every* temptation," suggests that the three described were part of a much wider range of soul struggle which is not disclosed. These three were only typical of what he endured. The departure of the

Devil from him "until an opportune time" also indicates that the struggle of Jesus is not over (4:13). It has just begun. The assaults of the Evil One continued throughout his ministry, for Jesus spoke of his disciples as "those who have continued with me *in my trials*" (22:28). The trials would be climaxed in Gethsemane's Garden (22:39-46) and on the cross (22:54—23:56). The glory of it all for us is that he now continues with us in *our* trials. "For because he himself has suffered and been tempted, he is able to help those who are tempted" (Heb. 2:18).

The Servant's Mission and Its Consequences (4:14-30)

The connection of this incident with what has gone before is clear. It is the testing in actual experience of the inner decision of Jesus made at the Temptation. How many have made high resolves in some moment of inner struggle, only to break down at the threshold of action! Will Jesus do the same?

What could be better designed as a test than the situation here? Jesus, the obscure son of a small village carpenter, has suddenly become famous "through all the surrounding country" (4:14). Now he returns to his home village and speaks in the synagogue. "The eyes of all in the synagogue were fixed on him" (vs. 20). They expect something wonderful from him, some sign that will demonstrate to them what has made him famous elsewhere. Behind their expectancy is the religious hope of deliverance from Rome, and the Messianic excitement kindled by John the Baptist. If Jesus was ever tempted to deny the decision made at the Baptism to be the obedient Servant of God, it was here! But what happens? Within a short time, his fellow villagers are seeking to kill him! Tested in action, he makes good. He will not compromise the decision of his soul to gain the favor of his people. He will be the obedient Servant, even at the risk of death.

For the Scripture reading and the comments to follow, Jesus chose Isaiah 61:1-2. There the prophet pictures the deliverance of Israel from exile in Babylon in terms of their Year of Jubilee. In this year all debts were cancelled, all slaves freed, and property went back to the original owner (Lev. 25). This was "good news to the poor" (4:18). So would be the release from Babylon, said the prophet. The captives would be freed, and those who had been shattered by enemy oppression would be released. They could return to the homeland with rejoicing. This would be

"the year of the LORD's favor," the year of grace (Isa. 61:2).
But the actual release from Babylonian captivity and the return
to the Holy Land had not brought the fulfillment for which they
hoped. Nor had the centuries since. Still they were an oppressed,
conquered, broken people. The prophet, then, must have had a
deeper meaning in mind. He must have been speaking of the
coming Messianic Age, when the *sin* which had led to the Babylonian captivity would be dealt with.

So, Jesus boldly links this Coming Age to himself. "Today
this scripture has been fulfilled in your hearing," he says (4:21).
Here we see that the heart of Jesus' message lay in the fact that
he was the fulfiller of the Old Testament. *Now* is God's gracious
time, for the One who is to usher it in is in their midst. All that
the prophets had announced, all that Jewish history prefigured,
was unrolling before their very eyes in him! There was a deeper
poverty, a worse captivity, a more tragic blindness, a more shattering oppression, than that of ancient Babylon or the Rome of
their day. It was that wrought by Satan. Here was the "stronger"
One who had come to invade Satan's domain and conquer him
(Luke 11:22). "The reason the Son of God appeared was to
destroy the works of the devil" (I John 3:8).

The initial response of the congregation was ambiguous. What
they had heard of him as a teacher, which they found hard to
believe in the light of their memories of him, was confirmed
(4:22). They were momentarily proud that such a gifted person
should have come from their village. But like the young Augus-
tine, who was impressed by the eloquence of Ambrose but indifferent to what he said, their admiration was purely superficial.
"Is not this Joseph's son?" they asked (vs. 22). How can he
make such claims for himself?

The one way Jesus' claims might be authenticated was to produce some miracles, as it was reported he had done in Capernaum (vs. 23). Here was the voice of the Tempter again. The
people were demanding exactly what Jesus had determined not
to do. His claims were not to be authenticated by a display of
signs, but by *faith*. The Scriptures were fulfilled in their "hearing," not by sight (vs. 21). God's word is heard; it calls for
faith. Men cannot demand of God that he send the Messiah in
the form they have predetermined. Faith cannot rest on visible
confirmation of a sort which the believer himself has determined.
(Note in Matthew 27:42 the later demand of the religious lead-

ers: "Let him come down now from the cross, and we will believe in him.") If the people of Nazareth refuse to believe his word, they will be placed in the same position as the ancient Israelites, who were considered by God to be less worthy of his grace than the Gentiles, such as the widow of Zarephath and Naaman the Syrian (vss. 25-27). Grace is given not on the basis of worthiness, but purely on the basis of faith (see Acts 13:46). The message of God's salvation is for all who "will listen" (Acts 28:28). At these words of Jesus, the people rose up in wrath and sought to kill him (vss. 28-29). It is plain why Luke, with Gentile readers in mind, stresses the universality of God's grace.

X

MESSIAH WORKS IN GALILEE: RESPONSE TO THE SERVANT

Luke 4:31—9:50

Thus far, Luke has given us his preface, his introduction, and his central theme. He now presents the Galilean ministry of Jesus in such fashion as to confront the reader with the various responses made to him. In the light of his purpose (see the Introduction and the discussion of 1:1-4), it is obvious that Luke is seeking to warn the reader against the wrong sort of response to Jesus, and to encourage him to make the right response. His purpose is not merely to tell how the people of Jesus' day responded to him. He faces the reader with the far more important question: What do *you* think of the Christ?

In doing this, three types of response are presented, one of which is central in each of the three parts which comprise this long section. The first is the *superficial acclaim* of the multitudes (4:31—5:26). Jesus' "mighty works" made a deep impression and created a tremendous stir, but did not lead to genuine faith or commitment on the part of many. The second response was that of outright *rejection* (5:27—6:11). Jesus so challenged the entrenched religious views of his time that the accredited leaders very early in his career set themselves to destroy him. What then? Admired by crowds who do not understand him, and hated by enemies who seek to destroy him, what course will he follow? Will he play on the emotions of the crowds, gaining a following whether they come to true faith or not? And as for his enemies, will he compromise with them to avoid a clash? Jesus does neither. He rather calls to himself the nucleus of the multitudes who are trying to penetrate more deeply into the mystery of his coming—"disciples," Luke calls them (6:13)—and from them chooses twelve Apostles around whom he may build a New Israel. These he patiently works with and teaches until at last they recognize him as their Messiah. This *growing insight of faith* on the part of those who finally confess him as the Christ, is the third type of response pictured by Luke (6:12—9:50).

Superficial Acclaim (4:31—5:26)

General Characteristics

This section is made up of a series of miracle stories. Jesus cast out demons, healed the sick, manifested his power over nature in the miraculous draft of fish, and forgave sin. Through frequent repetition, Luke indicates that these events were designed to show Jesus' "authority and power" (4:32, 36; 5:17, 24). His authority, however, was manifested not by magical incantations, occult ceremonies, or mysterious charms, but by his *word!* "His *word* was with authority" (4:32). He "rebuked" both demons and disease (4:35, 39, 41). The multitudes asked, "What is this *word?* For with authority and power he *commands* . . . " (4:36). Peter says, "At your *word* I will let down the nets" (5:5). By a *word* Jesus healed a leper (5:13) and forgave a man's sins (5:20). Here is one whose *word* carried authority over disease, nature, the world of demonic spirits, the human heart, and sin. In every realm where evil reigns, a mightier authority had come to intervene and to set men free. His authority resided in his Person. It was not the authority of the scribes, which lay in citing passages of Scripture or the tradition which had grown up around the Scriptures (Mark 1:22). It was an authority inherent in who Jesus himself was.

But there is no dwelling on the details of how Jesus' mighty deeds were done. The emphasis in each case is on the *response* which is made to them. The major interest in this section is on the superficial acclaim of the multitudes, which rises in an ever-growing crescendo of popularity for Jesus. "Reports of him went out into every place in the surrounding region" (4:37). When Jesus tried to stop this rising tide of almost hysterical enthusiasm, "so much the more the report went abroad concerning him"

(5:15). This led to the gathering of tremendous crowds who came from the whole countryside—some even from as far as Jerusalem—making it almost impossible for Jesus to teach them or for sick people to get near him (4:40, 42; 5:1, 15, 17-19).

The response of the multitudes was one of curiosity, interest, and desire to get from Jesus what they could. But it was not one of commitment or faith. They were "astonished" because of the authority of his teaching (4:32). They were "amazed" at his command of the unclean spirits (4:36). They were "filled with awe" at the strangeness of the things they had seen (5:26). But, like the people on Mount Carmel who remained noncommitted spectators when Elijah challenged them to decision (I Kings 18:21), there is no indication that they were minded to "follow" Jesus in the deepest sense. In fact, in a very subtle way, Luke suggests that the presence of the multitudes was really a repetition of the Temptation, where Jesus was faced with the decision between meeting the superficial needs of his people or being his Father's obedient Servant. When the crowds were at their height, "he withdrew to the wilderness and prayed" (5:16). He must fortify his soul once more against the temptation to succumb to the popular acclaim of those who did not understand his mission.

There are, however, two other strands of response here. Peter and his fellow fishermen "left everything and followed him" (5:11). On the other hand, the first opposition of the Pharisees is also introduced (5:21). Here are total commitment and the beginnings of total rejection. The latter of these will be developed in the next section (5:27—6:11). The former will become central in the following section (6:12—9:51).

Two difficult questions confront the modern reader about the materials now under consideration. The first is that of *demons*. It is easy for the modern mind, with its scientific bent, to look upon the idea of demons as a part of the ancient world view of the New Testament which is now outgrown, and to discard it. For the irreverent, the whole question is branded as superstition. Many believers try to see it as symbolic of *human* evil, and to salvage some religious meaning while discarding the form.

It is clear that the New Testament writers believed in demons. They carefully distinguished between demon possession and illness. Demons often manifested themselves in physical and psychic illnesses, such as dumbness (Luke 11:14), blindness (Matt. 12:22), epilepsy (Luke 9:39), and clairvoyance (Luke 4:34;

8:28). But to the New Testament writers, these manifestations of demon possession were not ordinary sicknesses. Luke makes a difference between Jesus' healing of "various diseases" and his casting out of demons (4:40-41). He also represents Jesus as distinguishing between authority over demons and the curing of diseases when he sent out the Twelve (9:1).

It is clear, too, that Jesus accepted the reality of demons. In fact, he used his authority over them as the final sign that he had brought the Kingdom of God (Luke 11:20). Either Jesus was accommodating himself to the superstitions of his day at this point, or was mistaken, or demons are real. The first is wholly unlikely. Jesus was quick to dispel superstition with regard to the cause of blindness (John 9:1-3). Furthermore, when he was accused of casting out demons by Beelzebub, he could have turned the argument by explaining that these were merely cases of illness, and had nothing to do with the unseen spirit world (Luke 11:15-26). Instead, he insisted that he had really cast out demons, and used this as evidence of his relation to God. It is hardly possible, then, to attribute Jesus' view of demons to accommodation.

Was he, then, mistaken? There can hardly be any doubt that he lived under the limitations of other men of his time so far as scientific knowledge is concerned. But in the realm of the spirit, where the deepest things of God, man, and evil are concerned, was he thus limited? We have not found him wrong about God or man. May it be that he was right, too, about demons?

Has modern science disproved the existence of demons? It has not, nor can it do so. Science necessarily deals with secondary causes and with the outward manifestations of disordered minds and bodies. What may lie behind these in the realm of unseen spiritual realities is not open to scientific proof or disproof. Categorically to deny the existence of demons may be to assume a range of knowledge about total reality which is not given to man.

To equate demon possession in the New Testament with superstition is difficult, in the light of the entire evidence. The gospel shattered superstition as light dispels darkness (see Acts 13: 6-11; 14:11-18; 16:16-18; 19:13-19; I Cor. 8:4-6; I Tim. 4:7). Granted that demons may be symbolic—since we must always think of suprahuman realms in human terms—yet may they not be *symbolic of suprahuman realities?* To Jesus and the New Testament writers, the disorder of the world was rooted in unseen, cosmic powers which were using human history as their sphere of action, but which were at war with God on a far grander scale than that (see II Cor. 11:14-15; Eph. 1:21; 3:10; 6:12; Col. 1:13, 16; 2:15; Heb. 2:14; I Peter 3:22). The casting out of demons, therefore, was a sign of Christ's Lordship over these cosmic powers. The fact that demon-possessed people knew him, that his presence created "torment" for them, suggests that their condition was more than an illness (see Luke 4:33-34; 8:28; Mark 3:11). Mental illness would not be worsened in the presence of Jesus; it would rather be quieted, if anything.

When Jesus approached a demon-possessed person, he was doing his work of attacking the stronghold of Satan to take "away his armor" and divide his "spoil" (Luke 11:22). If the struggle of the Temptation was a real encounter with Satan, it is not at all surprising that the demons knew who Jesus was. They had already met him, and already knew that he was the One through whom their destruction would come. To face him was to face their coming executioner. Is this symbolic? Yes, of necessity. But it is symbolic of realities, to deny which is to reduce the cosmic dimensions of the work of Christ, and limit his victory to a realm far less grand than that presented by the New Testament.

The second serious problem here is that of Jesus' *miracles*. In the light of science, is it possible to believe in miracles? Jesus' healing miracles are now accepted by many, because psychotherapy has demonstrated the tremendous influence of mind over body, and the power of suggestion in overcoming illnesses. But the nature miracles and the raisings from the dead are still suspect, for they cannot be accounted for on such grounds. This sort of reasoning, however, seems quite foreign to the New Testament. The New Testament writers conceived of sickness and the ravages of nature and death as evidences of the reign of Satan. With fiendish delight, exceeding that of modern brutish men who have their fellow men in their power, Satan tortures and racks his victims in countless ways before he destroys them (see Luke 13:16; Acts 10:38; II Cor. 12:7). The miracles of Jesus, therefore, were not skillful applications of the force of suggestion. They were rather evidences of divine "power" greater than the power of Satan (Luke 5:17). Jesus' miracles were signs of his Lordship over every realm where Satan had man in his grasp, and were a part of his battle which culminated in the Cross and Resurrection. They were foregleams of the process whereby "he disarmed the principalities and powers . . . triumphing over them" (Col. 2:15).

The miracles, however, were signs to faith only. The New Testament never seeks to prove Jesus' Lordship to the unbelieving by the fact that he did miracles. The deeper question always was: What do his miracles reveal about him? Are they signs that he has occult powers, or that he is demon-possessed? Or do they indicate that he is the One who has come to do battle with the kingdom of darkness and to establish the Kingdom of God? (see Luke 11:15-26). Many who saw his miracles and had no doubt about their reality still did not believe on him. Miracles are signs to faith, but do not produce faith. Furthermore, in the New Testament, they are always related to Jesus' teaching (see Luke 4:31-37; 5:1-11, 15). Jesus was no "wonder worker" who sought to command crowds and produce faith in himself by miracles. His miracles were outward signs of what he taught and of what he was. His works, his words, and his Person must never be separated. To appraise modern religious leaders by their power to do miracles has no relation whatsoever to the miracles of Jesus as set forth in the New Testament.

If Jesus' miracles were signs of his Lordship over the kingdom of Satan, then is it not God's will that Satan's works should be destroyed and that all men should be made well and safe in this world? Is it not a part of the gospel that God wills health and wholeness for everyone? In a broad sense one may answer "Yes" to these questions. All sickness and accident, just as all death, run counter to the will of God. It is his will "to destroy the works of the devil" (I John 3:8). It is false, however, to conclude from this that God wills health and safety immediately, here and now, for all men. This is to miss the meaning of Jesus' miracles as signs, and to fail to see the tension in the New Testament between what has "already" happened in Jesus and what has "not yet" taken place.

Jesus brought the Kingdom of God, and in the Cross and Resurrection triumphed over the works of Satan. But this triumph is not yet complete. Although "the kingdom of God has come" in Jesus (Luke 11:20), still we are commanded to pray, "Thy kingdom come" (Luke 11:2). Jesus "reigns" now (I Cor. 15:25), but "we do not yet see everything in subjection to him" (Heb. 2:8). God wills life for all his people, and the resurrection of Jesus is the sign that because he lives we shall live also (John

14:19). Yet we must die. We have the Holy Spirit, who is a pledge of our coming eternal life, but we "groan inwardly as we wait for . . . the redemption of our bodies" (Rom. 8:23).

If God wills to give the Church the signs of the coming Kingdom in miraculous healings of the sick, well and good. But we cannot force God's hand. Faith is no automatic guarantee of complete wholeness here and now. Believers, who have the Spirit, are still subject to the ravages of sickness, accident, storm, earthquake, and war, just as are unbelievers. It may well be that for many who are so cursed by the powers of darkness, God's answer will be what it was to Paul, not to remove the "thorn" but to do something better, to offer a sufficiency of grace which is made "perfect in weakness" (II Cor. 12:7-9). Jesus' miracles were the fulfillment of the Old Testament promises (see Luke 4:18-21; Matt. 8:17), but they were at the same time the promise of a coming fulfillment. We are saved in hope of that which we do not yet see, and wait "with patience" (Rom. 8:24-25).

A Day of Healing (4:31-44)

Capernaum was a trade center on the shores of the Sea of Galilee. Jesus went there from the more remote village of Nazareth to begin his announcement of the Kingdom of God on a wider scale (vs. 31). There, on a Sabbath day, he manifested his authority, both in teaching and in mastering unclean spirits (vss. 32-36). Jesus' presence produced a crisis. The demon recognized in Jesus his enemy, who would ultimately destroy him. Hence, he cried out in horror (vs. 33). This was the result of Jesus' holiness, inasmuch as the demon called him "the Holy One of God" (vs. 34). There can be nothing in common between absolute evil and absolute holiness. The fact that the demon recognized Jesus may well be explained from the fact of the encounter of Jesus with the Evil One at the Temptation (4:1-13). The word "us" may mean that the demon, speaking through the lips of his victim, classes them together, or it may refer to a multiplicity of demons in the man (see Luke 8:30).

Jesus' power over the demon lies not in incantations or magic, but solely in his *word* (vss. 35-36). A "command" from him is sufficient to master the demon. The visible convulsion as the demon departed shows the malice of the demon and his rebellion at being so summarily dismissed from his home (vs. 35). The fact that "no harm" was done to the man by this departing ges-

ture of the demon, suggests that Jesus is Lord even of the demonic resistance. In his presence, the Evil One is mastered.

Jesus' silencing of the demon's confession of his Messiahship
may be accounted for on two grounds. First, this was not a confession of true faith which could bear real witness to Jesus. It
was mere forced intellectual assent without religious value. James
pointed to the fact that "the demons believe—and shudder" as
the sort of faith which is worthless (James 2:19). Paul, like
Jesus, refused to tolerate any demonic testimony to his work
(Acts 16:16-18). The testimony of demons might awe or frighten
people. It could not lead them to a free commitment of their
lives to the saving deed of God's love in Christ. Second, the popular misconceptions of the Messiah abroad in Jesus' day made
it necessary for him to avoid any public announcement of his
Messiahship. This was his secret, later shared by his disciples,
who themselves did not fully understand it (Matt. 16:21-23),
to be proclaimed publicly only at Pentecost (Acts 2:36). But in
spite of Jesus' silencing the demon, still his authority over unclean spirits "amazed" the people, and "reports of him went out
into every place in the surrounding region" (Luke 4:36-37).

As Jesus had cast out the demon in the synagogue, he cast out
the fever of Simon's mother-in-law in the home with a "rebuke"
(4:39). In the light of Luke's later presentation of an ill person as
one "whom Satan bound" (13:16), it is quite likely that he here
looks upon disease as a work of Satan whose kingdom Jesus had
come to destroy (see also Acts 10:38). Here again is a sign that
Jesus is the "one stronger than he" who "assails him and over-
comes him" (Luke 11:22). The fact that the fever was "high"
and that the cured one "immediately . . . rose and served them"
(vs. 39), attests the power and the completeness of the cure.

Jewish law forbade the carrying of burdens on the Sabbath
(Jer. 17:21-22). At sunset, therefore, when the Sabbath ended,
the people brought to him their sick and demon-possessed. All
who came were healed, not in a mass healing but through individual attention—"he laid his hands on every one of them and
healed them" (vs. 40). To Jesus, individuals were never lost in
the crowd. The laying on of his hands was likely a gesture of
blessing (see Gen. 48:14; Mark 10:16), which was both a sign
of Jesus' interest in each individual and a possible aid to their
faith. There was no magic in this, for he could heal without it,
even at a distance (Luke 7:1-10). Again Luke distinguishes be-

tween Jesus' healings and his casting out of demons (vs. 41).

The purpose of Jesus' withdrawal to a "lonely place" (vs. 42) was, as Mark tells us, for prayer (Mark 1:35). Jesus' power to heal and to cast out demons was not automatic. It came from fellowship with his Father, continually renewed through prayer. Prayer was necessary, too, to keep him firm in his decision not to capitalize on the popularity with the masses which came through his mighty works. These works were signs that he had brought the Kingdom of God. They were the "good news" in action. As such, they were a part of the gospel. This is made very clear when the people seek him out and try to dissuade him from leaving. They are impressed by his wonders and would like him to do more. But Jesus replies, *"I must preach the good news of the kingdom of God* to the other cities also; for I was sent for this purpose" (vs. 43; italics added). Jesus had not come to be a mere wonder-worker, but to preach the good news of the Kingdom. And the miracles were a part of that good news! Those who saw only the wonders but did not see them as signs that Jesus had come to inaugurate the Kingdom of God, missed the point entirely.

The Miraculous Draft of Fish (5:1-11)

The broad shores of the Lake of Gennesaret (Sea of Galilee) offered a suitable place for open-air preaching. The people, however, came in such crowds and strained so eagerly to get within hearing and seeing distance, that Jesus was "pressed" almost into the water (vs. 1). By getting into Simon's boat, Jesus escaped the pressure of the crowd and gained a vantage point from which all could see and hear. What Jesus taught is not mentioned (vs. 3), for the emphasis of the story is on what happens afterward. It must have been, however, what it was on the earlier occasions— "the good news of the kingdom of God" (4:43).

To Simon, Jesus' command to "put out into the deep and let down your nets for a catch" (vs. 4) was laughable folly. Night-time was the time to fish, not the heat of the day. Furthermore, they had just fished all night and had taken "nothing"! It was useless to make another attempt at that time. Yet Peter had seen Jesus heal, and had just heard him preach. The "authority," therefore, both of his words and deeds, led Peter to obey his command, even though it ran counter to all his experience in a calling in which he was a master. "At your word I will" (vs. 5).

The result of Peter's obedient act was overwhelming (vss.

6-7). Whether this was a miracle of knowledge on Jesus' part, or whether the fish appeared there according to his will, we do not know, and it is immaterial. In any case, Peter interpreted the event as something which went beyond the mere human level, and he saw in Jesus One in whom God was active. He changed the address to Jesus from "Master" to "Lord," and fell prostrate before him (vs. 8). Like Isaiah when he caught a glimpse of divine holiness (Isa. 6), Peter had a sudden insight into the sinfulness of his own heart. This was so overwhelming that he seemed unable to endure the presence of Jesus, and cried out, "Depart from me."

What caused this response? The account does not say. It would, however, seem to have been caused by the overflowing grace which he had experienced from Jesus. Peter was an unworthy, sinful man, yet Jesus had entered his boat and, without being requested, had aided him to do what he had toiled for all night without success! He discovered what Paul wrote of later: "God's kindness is meant to lead . . . to repentance" (Rom. 2:4). It is significant that Peter's response to Jesus' miraculous dealing with him lay in the moral and spiritual realm. His attention was not riveted on the marvel. The marvel rather revealed that about Jesus' Person which made Peter see his own sinfulness. In this is seen the true meaning of Jesus' miracles. They were signs of the marvel of his Person.

Peter's instinctive recoil at the holiness of Jesus was met by Jesus' gracious words, "Do not be afraid" (vs. 10). Reverential fear, prompted by unworthiness, always leads to God's gracious acceptance. Only he who knows his unworthiness is worthy of Jesus' companionship. Much to Peter's surprise, Jesus calls him and his companions into permanent fellowship with him in his work. Out of the crisis of self-knowledge and faith comes the call to service. "Henceforth you will be catching men" (vs. 10). The word "catching" means to "capture alive," such as capturing animals for a zoo or taking prisoners alive in war. Its form suggests a continuous process. From now on, the continuous work of Peter and his companions will be to take men alive, to capture them for the Kingdom of God. To this task they gladly responded, leaving everything to follow him (vs. 11). The conditions on which Jesus can use men in his Kingdom are a willingness to work (vss. 2, 10), obedience to his commands (vs. 5), honesty about one's own unworthiness and sin (vs. 8), and a willingness to make whatever sacrifice his service demands (vs. 11).

Healing of a Leper (5:12-16)

Luke has arranged his materials in this section in ascending order, reaching a climax in the last verse (5:26). Would it not have been expected, then, that the incident of the healing of the leper should have been grouped with the healings in 4:31-44? The answer lies in the view of leprosy held in that time. Jesus' behavior toward this leper was more astounding to the crowds than his other healings, and produced an even greater stir (vs.15).

To the Jews, leprosy was more than a disease. It was a sign of moral uncleanness. It was a stroke of divine judgment for disobedience to the divine will (Num. 12; II Kings 5:19-27; II Chron. 26:16-21). Consequently, lepers were cast out of the congregation, not only as a hygienic measure but as a sign that they were cut off from fellowship with the people of God. They lived miserable existences, depending on alms of passers-by or on scavenging. Often, for mutual comfort and help they went about in groups (see II Kings 7:3; Luke 17:12).

This leper must have heard of Jesus' mighty works, for he came into the town in violation of the Law, and cast himself on the mercy of Jesus for help. He came with a strong measure of faith, assured that if Jesus were willing to do so, he was able to cure him (vs. 12). His hesitation over Jesus' willingness possibly lay in the fact that the moral uncleanness attributed to leprosy had conditioned him to doubt whether even God would be merciful to him. Since only two cases of healing were on record (Num. 12:9-15; II Kings 5:1-14), the rabbis taught that only God could heal leprosy (II Kings 5:7). A stroke of God could be lifted only by him! The confidence of the leper, then, shows clearly that he believed Jesus to have God's power.

Jesus' "touching" the leper was a violation of the ceremonial law. By this gesture, however, he indicated that no one was cut off from his fellowship. He had come not to withdraw from human need, but to be the "physician" to "those who are sick" (Luke 5:31). Yet Jesus had not come to "abolish" the Law. He had come rather to "fulfill" it (Matt. 5:17). And until men understood how grace was really the fulfilling of the Law on a higher level, the Law must be obeyed. Hence, Jesus bade the leper to keep silence about his healing, and to go to the priest to fulfill the law laid down in Leviticus 14. His offering there would prove that Jesus did not hold the Law lightly.

Also, since Jesus used his healing of lepers as a sign that in him the Kingdom had come (see Luke 7:22), it may be that the man's healed condition was to be a sign to the religious leaders in Jerusalem that the Messianic Age was here. Furthermore, Jesus' miracles were attracting too much publicity, which he sought to avoid. He hoped to achieve this end by sending the man silently away. Luke does not indicate, as does Mark, that the man disobeyed Jesus' orders and "began to talk freely about it, and to spread the news" (Mark 1:45). Yet Luke does say that the report "went abroad concerning him; and great multitudes gathered to hear and to be healed of their infirmities" (vs. 15). But Jesus "withdrew to the wilderness and prayed" (vs. 16; see also on 4:42).

A Paralytic Healed (5:17-26)

The story of the paralytic comes last in this section of the Gospel, as the climactic revelation of Jesus' authority and power. He has "authority on earth to forgive sins" (vs. 24). It is this claim which marks the beginning of open hostility to Jesus. The news of Jesus' teaching and works had created such a stir that "Pharisees and teachers of the law" had come all the way from Jerusalem to investigate (vs. 17). The Pharisees were the strict religious party in Judaism, who strongly opposed all outside influences on the Jewish faith, and rigorously insisted on absolute submission both to the Law and to the traditions of the elders which had grown up around it. They were the official interpreters of the Law, and had an almost absolute religious authority over the people. Hence, they felt quite capable of evaluating the work of Jesus, and either approving or condemning him.

The ordinary crowds were augmented on this occasion by the news that rabbis from Jerusalem were present, so that the friends of the paralyzed man could not get him to Jesus. Jesus was deeply impressed with the faith which led them to carry the paralytic on his pallet up to the roof and let him down (vs. 20). The content of the faith was probably the simple confidence that Jesus could heal the diseased victim.

Many see in Jesus' word, "Your sins are forgiven" (vs. 20), evidence that the man's illness had a direct connection with some specific sin, and that he needed forgiveness before he could have faith to be cured. There is nothing in the story to affirm or deny this hypothesis. The fact, however, that the cure seems to be made by Jesus' decision, and is not dependent on the man's faith so far as the record goes, makes the hypothesis doubtful. It is more likely that in the light of the great clamor for physical healing, and because of the presence of the religious leaders, Jesus is proclaiming by this act that he has come to do something deeper than physical healing. He has come to bring God's Kingdom, the central fact of which is the forgiveness of sins.

This was what led "the scribes and the Pharisees" to condemn Jesus (vs. 21). It was plain in the Scriptures that forgiveness of sins was the prerogative of God alone (Isa. 43:25; Pss. 32:2; 51:1-2, 9; 103:3). Here was a man claiming to do what only God could do. This was rankest blasphemy (vs. 21). And yet, if these religious leaders had been open to evidence, might they not have seen something deeper here? Was not the forgiveness of sins a sign of the Messianic Age? (see Isa. 40:2; Joel 2:32; Micah 7:18-19; Zech. 13:1). Could it not be that Jesus' words and deeds evidenced the inbreaking of the Day of Messiah?

To encourage them to think along these lines, Jesus used a logic which should have been convincing to them. It was easier to *say,* "Your sins are forgiven you," than it was to *say,* "Rise and walk" (vs. 23). No one could check on the former. The latter was open to examination. In order, therefore, to give them evidence that forgiveness had really taken place in the unseen realm, he gave them a visible sign to authenticate it by healing the man. Their own theology should have led them to accept this evidence. They blamed sickness on sin (see John 9:2), and said that there could be no healing until there was forgiveness. On the grounds of their own theology the healing of the man was evidence that forgiveness had taken place. Then, too, if Jesus had presumed to forgive sins without the right to do so, he would have been a blasphemer and would thereby not have had the power of God. When, therefore, he showed God's power in the healing of the man, was that not evidence that he was no blasphemer, but God's Messiah, and therefore had "authority on earth to forgive sins"? (vs. 24).

For the first time in this Gospel, Jesus calls himself "the Son of man" (vs. 24). This expression is first found in Daniel, where "one like a son of man" is given dominion over all peoples in an everlasting kingdom "that shall not be destroyed" (7:13-14). In the Intertestament period this figure had been emphasized and given a Messianic interpretation. The expression, however, did not have the political overtones of the term "Messiah," from which Jesus shrank. It seemed to be the Messianic designation least likely to provoke his followers to political revolution against Rome. It also furnished Jesus with an indirect title of Messiahship, which could well arouse spiritual curiosity and thus lead men further into an understanding of him.

The climax of this whole section is in the response of amazement, praise, and awe made by the people. "We have seen strange [or, paradoxical] things today," they said (vs. 26). Things seemed contradictory. A paralytic walked. A man forgave sins. But did they understand? They were impressed, but not convinced. There was amazement, but no faith. In a profound sense, with the people Jesus was defeated by his very success.

Oct. 20

Rejection (5:27—6:11)

General Characteristics

In this section, Luke selects materials which bring out the opposition of the religious leaders to Jesus. The popular crowds are still present, as are the disciples, but "the Pharisees and their scribes" definitely take the center of the stage (5:30, 33; 6:2, 7). The choice of materials brings out clearly certain basic issues over which Jesus and his enemies differed, and shows that no compromise between them is possible. Jesus' "new wine" cannot be poured into the "old wineskins" (5:37). There is something revolutionary here which is too vital to be contained in the rigid forms which Judaism had produced.

It is well to note that the major point at issue is the meaning of the Old Testament. The "newness" of Jesus is not wholly new in the sense that it has no roots. It is rather a "new" way of looking at the Old Testament. The Pharisees and their scribes were doctors of the Law, experts in the Scriptures. Jesus' sharpest challenge lay in his insistence that they did not understand the Scriptures, and had missed the will of God revealed there.

Three issues dear to the hearts of the Pharisees are brought into the open—eating with the morally unworthy, fasting, and Sabbath observance. At first, the Pharisees take the offensive against Jesus (5:30, 33; 6:2). Finally, however, Jesus seems deliberately to confront them with the issue which lay between them by healing a man under circumstances which he knew would offend them, and by taking the initiative in discussing it (6:6-11). He who brought the Kingdom shatters even our best religious pretensions, and shows that our highest virtues are often idols set in the place of God. We may either accept this shattering as a part of God's mercy in leading us to himself, or resist in self-will and refuse his grace. The Pharisees chose the latter course. They began with "murmuring" and seeking an "accusation" against Jesus (5:30; 6:7). With ever-increasing resistance they ended in "fury," determined to destroy him (6:11).

Feasting with Sinners (5:27-32)

The story grows quite naturally out of the incident preceding it. There Jesus was presented as the One who has power to free men from sin (5:24). Here he is seen at work mastering one of the most difficult forms of sin—slavery to riches. Levi (Matthew, see Matt. 9:9) was a "tax collector." Since he was "sitting at the tax office" (5:27), it is quite likely that he had charge of the customs collections on the trade route which passed near to Capernaum. In this position, he had opportunity to enrich himself, especially at the expense of the poor, who would not know the laws and could not well defend themselves against official corruption. Tax collectors were deeply hated by the Jews, especially by the Pharisees, as traitors and religiously depraved people. In contrast to the Pharisees, who had religious dealings only with the "righteous," Jesus not only had fellowship with Levi but called him into special service in his Kingdom. Luke's statement that he left "everything" suggests the great possessions Levi had to give up to follow Jesus (vs. 28). Here we see Jesus' power to conquer the strong claim which riches make on men.

In celebration of his new-found faith and to introduce his friends to his Lord, Levi invited Jesus to a great banquet in his home (vs. 29). The size of the group of guests indicates that Levi's home was large, and his resources ample. The Pharisees, who by now were watching every opportunity to amass evidence against Jesus, came in during the dinner, probably uninvited. At oriental feasts, uninvited guests often stand around the edges as mere spectators of the proceedings. The Pharisees were shocked by what they saw. In the East, table fellowship is the sign of full acceptance. To eat with another marks him as worthy of one's fellowship. Here was Jesus, who claimed to be the bringer of

God's Kingdom, at table with men of evil life. The Pharisees registered their protest with the disciples (vs. 30). Jesus, aware that he was being watched, answered the charge.

His answer was simple, yet profound. He had come to proclaim the grace of God to men (4:19). Where should he go with this proclamation but to those who needed it—to sinners? He was the physician of the soul who must go to those who were sick, not to those who were well (vs. 31). He did not, of course, mean that there were really any spiritually well, who did not need him. He was ironically referring to the Pharisees who *thought* they were well, who believed they were already favorites of God, because they tried scrupulously to keep the external matters of the Law. Since they felt no need, there was nothing Jesus could do for them. He had come to call "sinners to repentance" (vs. 32), and it was only those who knew that they were sinners who would hear his voice.

Fasting (5:33-39)

Fasting was not an obligatory religious rite for the Jews. It had, however, become customary with the Pharisees to fast twice in the week (Luke 18:12). John the Baptist also had imposed fasting on his disciples (vs. 33). Fasting was habitually accompanied by prayer (see 2:37). Jesus had prescribed no fasting for his disciples. This, coupled with his free fellowship with those of doubtful life (5:29), led the Pharisees to look upon him as a libertine. They therefore brought their protest.

Jesus' initial answer was another proclamation—if they had ears to hear it—that the Messianic Age had come. He said that if his disciples should fast at that time, it would be as inappropriate as fasting at a wedding. A wedding is a time of rejoicing, of feasting, not of fasting. What lay behind this answer? In Jewish thought, a wedding feast had become a picture of the Messianic Age. Hosea had spoken of the final redemption as a "betrothal" between God and his people (Hosea 2:19-20). John the Baptist had taken up this figure by referring to Jesus as the "bridegroom" and himself as "the friend of the bridegroom" (John 3:29). Jesus used the picture of a "marriage feast" in speaking of the Kingdom (Matt. 22:2-10; 25:1-13). The Christians later spoke of the Church as the "bride" of Christ (Rev. 19:7; 21:2; see also Eph. 5:21-33). Jesus' reply to their question, therefore, was really a proclamation. It would be inappropriate for his disciples to fast, for the "bridegroom" is here. This is a time of rejoicing, for the Kingdom has come!

Jesus added a word, however, which hints strongly of his death. "The days will come, when the bridegroom is taken away from them, and then they will fast in those days" (5:35). A deeper mourning will come then than the Pharisees now know (see John 16:20). But the Resurrection will turn even that sorrow into joy. Henceforth, even the yearning of the Church for the full and final coming of the Kingdom, expressed in the prayer "Thy kingdom come," will be a yearning mingled with joy in the full confidence of its coming. Christians are to rejoice even in "sufferings" (Rom. 5:3; James 1:2, 12; see also Luke 6:22-23).

The inappropriateness of fasting when Jesus was here, therefore, does not rule out fasting entirely. When Jesus was here, the Kingdom was present. But in the period between his death and his Final Coming, the Kingdom, though present, is not here in its fullness. Fasting, therefore, may again be appropriate in the life of the Church as a sign of desire for the final coming of the Kingdom, and as a spontaneous self-discipline undertaken to keep the joy of the Kingdom bright, and to make it possible to share one's goods with the needy (see Isa. 58:1-12).

From fasting, Jesus turns to a broader application of the truth of which he has been speaking. The coming of the Messiah has brought such a radical change that it must find new forms in which to express itself. To try to patch up the old forms would be like tearing a piece from a new garment and sewing it onto an old one. In this way, the patch stands out in ugly fashion on the old garment, and the new garment is also ruined. The old garment of Judaism must be laid aside now for the new garment of the gospel. In fact, the principle of life stirring in the gospel is so strong that it would shatter the old forms of Judaism, as the fermentation of new wine would break old and inelastic wineskins. To try to pour the new life into the old forms would be both to ruin the old forms and to lose the new life (vss. 36-39).

The Sabbath (6:1-11)

Jesus, on several occasions, broke the tradition of the Pharisees by healing on the Sabbath (6:1-11; see also 13:10-17; 14:1-6). His action seems to have been a deliberate challenge to their tradition, for in each instance those whom he healed were chronic cases whose condition might well have gone another day with-

out disaster. Jesus apparently chose to challenge the Sabbath tradition because it furnished an excellent illustration of how far the
religious leaders had missed the will of God as revealed in the Old
Testament. The strictness with which the Sabbath was observed
was a point of pride with the Pharisees. The Sabbath was considered the most valuable treasure of Judaism, next to the Temple.

In the Old Testament, the Sabbath was related both to creation
(Gen. 2:2-3; Exod. 20:8-11; 31:12-17) and redemption (Deut.
5:12-15). It was a weekly reminder that the God who had created the universe was present with them, and that he had given
them rest by redeeming them from their bondage in Egypt.
Hence, the Law read: "The seventh day is a sabbath to the LORD
your God; in it you shall not do any work" (Exod. 20:10). The
purpose of the Sabbath law was glory to God. The *means* was
cessation from work. The Pharisees, however, had forgotten the
purpose, and had turned the means into an end. *To do no work*
was to keep the Sabbath! The glory of God was forgotten.
Hence, the Sabbath had become a day of prohibitions, many of
which were laughable. Work had to be defined. It was divided
into thirty-nine categories, each of which was broken down further. To keep the Sabbath rightly, therefore, one had to remember dozens of specific rules about things not to do!

The Law specifically forbade harvesting on the Sabbath (Exod.
34:21). The Pharisees, therefore, interpreted the spontaneous
and innocent act of Jesus' disciples in plucking grain as harvesting (Luke 6:1-2). Jesus' reply was twofold. First, he reminded
them of the occasion on which David had eaten the holy bread
in the House of God, and had given it to his companions (I Sam.
21:1-6). This was forbidden in the Law, because the holy bread
was for the priests only (Lev. 24:5-9). Here the Scriptures themselves allowed an exception to the Law. A higher law was imposed on the ceremonial law—the law of human need.

This in itself would have been a sufficient reply to the charge
of Sabbath breaking. But there is much more involved. It was
David who had done this. And Messiah was the Son of David!
In Jesus' justification of his action on the basis of David, he was
really saying, *I* have the right to do this, for I am David's Son!
Therefore, what was right for David's companions is lawful for
my disciples. With his usual avoidance of the term "Messiah,"
he made this implication more clear by saying, "The Son of man
is lord of the sabbath" (6:5). We have already seen that the pur-

pose of the Sabbath was to remind the people of the presence of God and of his redemption. The initial redemption at the Exodus was not sufficient. The real redemptive "rest" to which God was leading them would come only in the Messianic Age (see Heb. 3:7—4:10). By claiming Lordship over the Sabbath, therefore, Jesus was declaring that the Messianic Age had come. God is now present in him! The "rest" which God had promised was the redemption which Jesus had brought! God had ceased from his work of creation, but he was active in his work of redemption, even on the Sabbath. For Jesus to work redemptively on that day, therefore, was a sign that the Messianic Age had dawned in him. To keep the Sabbath rightly was not to memorize rules of what not to do. It was to enter into the freedom and joy of fellowship with him. Jesus was not setting aside the Sabbath law. He was rather fulfilling it.

On another occasion, Jesus took the initiative in pressing the Sabbath question (6:6). He knew that he was being officially "watched" by the Pharisees, in order that they might "find an accusation against him" (vs. 7). One can almost feel the concentrated silence as the man whom he called rose to his feet, stepped to the front of the synagogue, and stood before Jesus. Then Jesus posed a question: "I ask you, is it lawful on the sabbath to do good or to do harm, to save life or to destroy it?" (vs. 9).

The Pharisees could not answer this question without condemning themselves. Even they made exceptions to the Sabbath law in order to help one who was in danger of death. Was God interested only in keeping people from dying? Did not concern over life mean concern over wholeness of life as well? And if the Sabbath was made for God's glory, was it not a proper use of it to bring health to one of his children? After looking each of them in the eye (vs. 10), Jesus restored the man's withered hand. In this way, he was showing in action what he later phrased in words, when he said that all the Law and the Prophets were gathered up in love to God and to one's neighbor (see Matt. 22:37-40; Luke 10:25-28). These two laws take precedence over all lesser laws. The proper observance of the Sabbath, then, is not negative harmlessness, but positive service to God and to man.

While Jesus was "saving" life on the Sabbath, they were using the Sabbath to take counsel how they might "destroy" him. They were so filled with "fury" that their reason was temporarily upset (vs. 11). They could not introduce this new wine into their old wineskins. To save all that was precious to them, they must get rid of Jesus. Their views and his could not exist together. One can already hear the gathering rumble of the later cry, "Away with this man . . . Crucify, crucify him!" (23:18, 21).

The Growing Insight of Faith (6:12—9:50)

General Characteristics

Luke has given us a section in which the crowds were central (4:31—5:26), followed by another in which hostility was the major feature (5:27—6:11). Attention shifts now to a third group, the *disciples*. These were the ones in the multitudes who were avowed followers of Jesus, who had committed themselves to him within the limits possible at that time. Although the crowds are still present, Luke makes a careful distinction between them and the disciples. He mentions "a great crowd of his disciples *and* a great multitude of people" (6:17); "his disciples *and* a great crowd" (7:11). Jesus told his first parable to "a great crowd" but "his disciples" asked him what it meant (8:4, 9).

But there is an even greater narrowing of interest. From his disciples, Jesus called *twelve* to be Apostles (6:13). Surrounded by crowds who admired but misunderstood him, and dogged by enemies who were set to destroy him, Jesus here founded a New Israel, to be "built upon the foundation of the *apostles*" as well as the prophets (Eph. 2:20). The Old Israel had rejected him (6:11). He therefore called twelve Apostles, who would take the place of the twelve tribal fathers of the Old Israel. Out of these a New Israel would grow, who would fulfill the destiny of the Old Israel to be "a chosen race, a royal priesthood, a holy nation, God's own people" (I Peter 2:9). The number of times this group is mentioned in this section indicates clearly that they are central in the author's interest (8:1, 22; 9:1, 10, 12, 18, 40, 43, 46, 49). And even when they are not mentioned, they are in the background, watching Jesus at work and absorbing his teaching, as their confession of him clearly indicates (9:20). There is an even greater narrowing of interest in two places, where Peter, John, and James are singled out from the Twelve for special attention (8:51; 9:28). Instruction of the disciples in the true nature of his mission was such a delicate task that not even all of the Twelve at this stage were ready for it.

The climax of this section is the combination of the Great Confession (9:20), the first announcement of Jesus' suffering (9:22, 44), and the Transfiguration (9:28-36). Like the Baptism-Temptation experience, these are all parts of one whole, which can be understood only as they are taken together. Luke prepares the reader for this climax by indicating that there was a growing necessity for some explanation of Jesus. The climax is the answer to the question, "Who?" (9:18, 20).

This question is introduced several times. The Forerunner sends to Jesus, asking, "Are you *he who is to come,* or shall we look for another?" (7:19). Guests at Simon's dinner rather contemptuously ask, *"Who* is this, who even forgives sins?" (7:49). The disciples say one to another: *"Who* then is this, that he commands even wind and water, and they obey him?" (8:25). Superstitious Herod asks in perplexity: "John I beheaded; but *who* is this about whom I hear such things?" (9:9). All of this leads up to the climax, where Jesus asks the disciples: *"Who* do the *people* say that I am?" (9:18). Then he clinches it all with the decisive question: "But *who* do *you* say that I am?" (9:20).

It is an interesting study to trace back through the whole section to see what it was that led the disciples to make a different reply from that of the people. The impact of Jesus' Person through their intimate fellowship with him, the impact of his works and words, and the result of their experience in work for him (9:1-6)—these, interpreted by faith, led to their confession. But behind these there is the abiding mystery of grace, without which no one can confess Jesus as Lord (I Cor. 12:3).

The Call of the Apostles (6:12-16)

The seriousness of choosing the twelve Apostles is indicated by Jesus' all-night prayer session in preparation for it (6:12). They were the foundation of the New Israel, and it was imperative that they be chosen in accord with the will of God. In Jesus' day, the term "apostle" meant a representative sent by another to act in his name. That is why Jesus could say, "He who hears you hears me, and he who rejects you rejects me, and he who rejects me rejects him who sent me" (10:16). The Apostles were appointed to act in the name and in the power of Jesus after his death (Acts 1:8). The only organizational acts of Jesus were the choice of the Apostles and the giving of the Sacraments. The rest he left to his Apostles following the Resurrection.

The Apostolate included all sorts of men—fishermen, tax collectors, Zealots who had formerly taken the sword against Rome,
leaders as well as followers, men of action and men of thought,
ready believers and questioners, Galileans and Judeans, even one
"who became a traitor" (vs. 16). Why Judas was called will
likely forever remain a mystery. The wide variety in Jesus' choice
suggests his interest in all sorts of men. It also indicates that the
Church is made up of all types of people, whose sole reason for
fellowship is their common attachment to him. No congregation
made up merely of like-minded people who band together by
their own choice is a real church. On the other hand, because of
diversities of temperament, gifts, background, interests, and outlook, no congregation *could* remain together save by the oneness
which they find in Jesus.

The Law of the Kingdom (6:17-49)

Having pictured the New Israel which is to succeed the Old
Israel, Luke now proceeds to present some of the teaching of
Jesus which might be considered the law of the Kingdom to
which the New Israel is to bear witness. The New Israel, the
Church, is not itself the Kingdom. Its mission is to bear witness
to the Kingdom which Jesus has brought, and will bring in its
fullness in the future. The ethical teachings here set forth, therefore, are to be understood in the light of Jesus' proclamation of
the Kingdom. They are not mere principles of good behavior set
forth like those of other ethical teachers. Were they that, they
would be only our condemnation, for no one can measure up to
the demands of this law. The law of the Kingdom must not be
separated from the King of the Kingdom! It was given by the
only One who fully obeyed it.

The sermon here is a partial collection of the materials in
Matthew's Sermon on the Mount. In line with his purpose, Luke
omits much of purely Jewish interest (for example, Matt. 5:
17—6:18). Other parts of Matthew's collection Luke scatters
throughout his Gospel. It is quite likely that Luke gives more
nearly the original setting of the various teachings, while Matthew collects them by subjects. It has been remarked that Matthew
is like a florist arranging bouquets, while Luke is like a naturalist
who prefers to study his flowers in their native habitat.

The Beatitudes are fewer in number than those of Matthew,
and are followed by corresponding woes which are there lacking

(vss. 20-26; see Matt. 5:3-12). The woes serve to reinforce the seriousness of Jesus' teaching. The difference in form between Matthew and Luke is more apparent than real. Jesus spoke in Aramaic. Matthew and Luke give Greek translations. Luke probably translates literally, Matthew figuratively. Basically, they mean the same thing. Jesus was not pronouncing blessing on poverty, hunger, weeping, and social ostracism in themselves. It was only as these were incurred through discipleship to him, "on account of the Son of man" (vs. 22), that they brought blessing. Nor was Jesus pronouncing a curse on riches, abundance, laughter, and social acceptance in themselves. It was only as these came merely from the "good things" of this world (see Luke 16:25), and made men content with their own lives instead of seeking fellowship with God, that they were accursed. So poverty of spirit, hungering after righteousness, weeping over one's sin, social exclusion for the sake of Christ—these are the sources of blessing. For many they may well mean literal poverty, hunger, and tears. But neither abundance nor lack comes into question here, apart from its relation to membership in the Kingdom of God. To be satisfied with this world alone, without any yearning for the world to come, is to come to ultimate woe (see Luke 12:16-21; 16:19-31).

The heart of the Law of the Kingdom is love. Christian love is not to be confused with sentiment, a way of feeling. It is rather the will in action for the good of others. Love is, therefore, the opposite of self-centeredness, which is the law of this world estranged from God. To show how thoroughgoing this love is, Jesus commanded, "Love your enemies" (vs. 27). Sentiment might motivate members of the kingdoms of this world to self-effacement for those they love. But Christian love is the denial of the self in the interests even of enemies who hate and curse. The positive nature of such love is to be seen in the fact that the Christian is to "do good," "bless," and "pray" for his enemies (vss. 27-28). Love is not mere passive acceptance of affronts, but positive, aggressive action designed to redeem those who offend.

Four illustrations are given to make this concrete (vss. 29-30). These are, of course, not to be understood as rules to be followed literally on all occasions. They must be interpreted in terms of love, which wills the good of others. It would not be good always to turn the other cheek, and give to beggars. But when resistance must be given or punishment meted out, it should not be the result of the self-centeredness which is prompted by one's own desires, but because it is in the interests of the offender. The measure by which self-interest is to be reversed in the Kingdom is always to place one's self in the position of the other, and act toward him as we would desire if we were in his place (vs. 31). How radical this is may be known only by those who have tried it in a situation where self-interest is involved!

The motivation of Christian love is rooted in God's love for us (vss. 32-36). Love in order to get love, goodness for the sake of receiving goodness, lending in the hope of gain—these are manifestations of self-interest which have no place in the Christian life. Why? Because God is "kind to the ungrateful and the selfish" (vs. 35). Those who "will be sons of the Most High" should imitate him. "Be merciful, even as your Father is merciful" (vs. 36). God's mercy to us is the ground of our mercy to others. He who refuses mercy to others knows neither the depth of God's mercy nor his own unworthiness (see Matt. 18:23-35).

The section on love is concluded by a negative and a positive illustration of its practical outworking. Judge not, condemn not, is the prohibition (vs. 37). Why? Because God alone is Judge. If we, in his mercy, have been "acquitted" by forgiveness of our sins, it ill behooves us to manifest a spiritual superiority to others in judging them. God alone knows the hearts of men, knows all the circumstances which have contributed to an act, knows all the influences which have molded men's behavior, is able rightly to judge responsibility and to impart forgiveness. It is, therefore, not only a violation of love to judge a brother. It is usurpation of a divine prerogative! (James 4:12). This is incongruous in those whose discipleship involves accepting the final Lordship of God, and whose sole motivation should be gratitude for undeserved forgiveness (see again Matt. 18:23-35!). This does not mean that moral judgment of issues is to be obliterated. It means that one's judgment should not shift from issues to persons.

The positive aspect of this is to forgive, and to give freely (vss. 37-38). These are not to be done *in order* that we may be forgiven and may receive, but *because* we have already been forgiven and have already received God's bounty. God's grace may flow freely toward us only when we are channels through which it may flow to others (see Matt. 6:14-15; 18:35; Mark 11:25; Eph. 4:32; Col. 3:13; James 2:13). Graciousness to a brother shows that we have received grace from God.

The thought now turns to the responsibility of disciples toward others. To become a disciple is to be obliged to lead others to discipleship. Since one will not often lead another deeper into the faith than he himself has gone (vs. 40), it is necessary for him to take care to be at his best. If one is blinded by spiritual pride and by a failure to understand his own situation as a sinner under the judgment of God, albeit a "forgiven" sinner, he will be nothing more than a blind man leading blind men to disaster (vs. 39). To try to exercise moral authority over others without first having subjected one's self to the most careful moral judgment, is like trying to remove a "speck" from the eye of another with a "log" in one's own eye (vss. 41-42). Religious people are prone to get deeply disturbed by relatively unimportant moral defects in others, while being blinded to glaring faults in themselves. The cure for this is the awareness of the enormity of one's own sin before God, and the wonder of his grace that accepts us in spite of the "log" in our eye. In the light of this, we shall deal with the "speck" in our brother's eye not as his judge (vs. 37), but for his healing.

It is especially important, therefore, that one keep his inner life open to God for his continual cleansing and renewing. For our "words" to others can only express what we are within (vss. 43-45). There is a divine law, well illustrated in nature, that fruit corresponds to the quality of the tree on which it grows. It is possible to use words which belie the inner condition of the heart. In the long run, however, such words become like a "noisy gong or a clanging cymbal" (I Cor. 13:1). A true heart is the only effective means of true service for God.

What is a true heart? It is the disposition to obey. True discipleship is the glad acknowledgment of Christ's Lordship. And this acknowledgment lies in obedience. It is not enough to call Jesus Lord with the lips. One must own his Lordship with an obedient life—"do what I tell you" (vs. 46; see James 1:22-25; Ezek. 33:30-33). Whether one's acknowledgment of Jesus' Lordship is only in word or is in reality will be revealed by the crises of life. If one stands when floods of trouble arise for the sake of Christ, his discipleship has been real. But if not—the "ruin" is "great" (vs. 49). It may be that in the background of the picture here is the Last Judgment, when "all are open and laid bare to the eyes of him with whom we have to do" (Heb. 4:13). The reader is left with the seriousness of this sounding in his ears.

The Centurion's Servant (7:1-10)

Capernaum was a border town, between Galilee—ruled at that time by Herod Antipas—and the territory of his brother Philip (3:1). The centurion mentioned in the story was likely in charge of the border guard in the employ of Antipas rather than of the Romans. The fact that he sent Jews to intercede for him (vs. 3), and that Jesus contrasts his faith with that of "Israel" (vs. 9), indicates that he was a Gentile. He was probably a "God-fearer," who had been attracted to Judaism by its monotheism and high ethical teaching, and who even worshiped at the synagogue, but had not been circumcised as a proselyte (see Acts 16:14; 17:4). It seems to have been through the Jews that the centurion heard of Jesus and his work (vs. 3). He was a man of generous and compassionate nature (vss. 5 and 2).

Word of Jesus' coming convinced the centurion of his willingness to help. Humility and a sense of unworthiness led him to send friends to Jesus to tell him that he need not bother coming to his house. If Jesus would only speak the word of healing, his servant would recover (vss. 6-7). His confidence in the authority of Jesus' word evinced a remarkable faith. As a soldier he knew the effect of authoritative commands. When his superiors ordered, he obeyed. When he ordered, his subordinates obeyed (vs. 8). This reveals his faith in Jesus' authority. He believed that if Jesus commanded the disease to depart, his word would be obeyed. The stress of the story lies less on the healing of the servant (vs. 10) than on the centurion's faith (vs. 9). It is significant that the first incident Luke records after the forming of the New Israel and the setting forth of its Law (6:12-49), presents a Gentile manifesting the sort of faith which makes one a member of it. "So you see that it is men of faith who are the sons of Abraham" (Gal. 3:7).

The Raising of the Widow's Son (7:11-17)

In this story, death is seen at its worst. It had struck youth, claiming its prey long before the lad had lived out a normal span. Death could conceivably be a mercy in old age. But here death had struck a particularly vicious blow, taking the only son of a widow (vs. 12). Widows in that day were pitiable in any case, for they had no legal rights, and could not receive any inheritance. They were dependent on their sons, or the relatives of their husbands, whose support could not be legally demanded. The death of her son had left the widow defenseless in a cruel world. With no male heir, the family name would be cut off in Israel. Here is the tragedy of humanity at its worst. The widow's tears were eloquent testimony to the lordship of death.

Jesus' final battle with death was yet to come. It would come in the Cross and the Resurrection. The restoring of the young man, therefore, did nothing to solve the problem of death, for he would have to die again. Jesus seems to have acted here purely out of compassion for the mother (vs. 13). There is no display, no dramatic calling attention to what he is doing—merely an authoritative word which calls the young man back to life, and the simple statement: "And he gave him to his mother" (vs. 15).

The response of the crowd was twofold: fear, which unusual tokens of the presence of God always awaken; and praise to God (vs. 16). "God has visited his people" in the form of "a great prophet." Two Old Testament prophets had restored dead sons to their mothers (I Kings 17:17-24; II Kings 4:18-37). Now God was acting again through a prophet. But Luke intends to suggest that, although Jesus did not do this miracle for the purpose of proclaiming his Messiahship, yet it was a sign that in him the Kingdom of God had drawn very near.

For the first time, Luke calls Jesus "Lord" (vs. 13). This was the favorite description of Jesus in the Early Church, and corresponds to the name for God in the Old Testament. Although the crowds saw only a "prophet" at work, the Twelve must have seen something more. Surely this event was a major factor in bringing them to confess Jesus as the Messiah (9:20).

This event has been explained by some as the awakening of the young man from a trance, and by others as a mere story symbolic of the spiritual resurrection which Jesus brings. If the first were true, one would have expected Jesus to enlighten the people on the evils of premature burial! The second is wholly contrary to the nature of the Gospel, which purports to be presenting *events,* not symbolic stories (1:1). There is no question that the Early Church looked upon this as historic event. In the light of their view of his Person, this was no problem. In spite of our scientific knowledge which they did not have, the final question for us is whether we share their understanding of Jesus' Person.

The Baptist's Question (7:18-35)

John's problem arises from the report of his disciples brought to him in prison (vs. 18). This report is the judgment of the people which has spread throughout the country (vs. 17). "A great prophet has arisen among us!" (vs. 16). A "great prophet"? John had announced Jesus as more than a prophet (3:15-17). He himself was the forerunner of the promised Messiah. Jesus, therefore, was to baptize with the Holy Spirit. He would purge Judaism of its unfruitful members. He would bring God's harvest, when the wheat would be gathered into the granary and the chaff burned (3:9, 17). Now, John is not so sure.

Attempts have been made to lift any element of doubt from John, by suggesting that he sent his disciples to Jesus for their sake, or that he was impatient for Jesus to manifest himself and was urging him to do so. It is better to take the story at face value. Jesus' answer was made to John, not to his disciples. Furthermore, the rebuke of verse 23 suggests that Jesus sensed in John's question a real lack of understanding.

Other Old Testament leaders had their weak moments (Num. 20:12; I Kings 19:4; Jer. 20:14-18). Why, then, was it not possible that John should have doubted? Jesus was not fulfilling the program John had set up for him. He had not purged Israel, nor shown his power against Israel's enemies. He was doing only what earlier prophets had done, healing and raising the dead. Furthermore, the people did not share John's earlier judgment, for they saw in Jesus only a prophet. Then, too, John was in prison, and Jesus had done nothing to rescue him. Yes, John's question was poignant and real. "Are you he who is to come, or shall we look for another?" (vs. 19).

Jesus' reply, in effect, was to tell John to examine what he was doing and teaching—"what you have seen and heard" (vs. 22)—in the light of the Old Testament. Jesus' description of his work was taken from the prophecy of Isaiah (Isa. 29:18-19; 35:5-6; 61:1). He was telling John that he was fulfilling what the prophet had written of the Messianic Age. John would have to examine the evidence, and believe. There is no direct, authoritarian answer which Jesus would make. Faith is insight, not credulity. Jesus ends with an appeal for personal trust in himself (vs. 23).

Jesus' interpretation of John's ministry was intended to throw light on his own. John was in prison and was soon to die. The significance of his ministry now lay in the response of the people to Jesus, whom John had announced. They would not have followed John to the wilderness if he had been a weak or merely sensational man (vss. 24-25). No, John was a true prophet, and more than a prophet. It was he whom Malachi had described as the one who should prepare God's people for the Messianic Age (vss. 26-27). By virtue of his position as the last of the pre-Christian prophets, who was privileged to announce the immediate arrival of the New Age, John had the most important position in the unfolding of God's plan until that time. But the Kingdom which Jesus had come to establish was so much superior to all that had gone before, that the very least in it would be more privileged than John (vs. 28).

Verses 29 and 30 are considered by many to be a comment inserted in the midst of Jesus' remarks. It is difficult to know. In any case, these verses indicate a twofold response to the ministry of John, which is paralleled in the response to Jesus (vss. 36-50). The response of rejection is in no way the fault of God, but is solely the fault of unbelieving men. In God's providence, John came with an ascetic life and a message of judgment, and was rejected as having been demonically inspired. Jesus, on the other hand, came with a wholly different method, and was accused of gluttony (vss. 33-34). The fault lay in those who rejected them, whom Jesus describes as petulant children who refuse to play, whether the game be wedding or funeral (vss. 31-32). But God's wisdom is vindicated in the fact that there were those who heard both John and Jesus, and were responding to the inbreaking of the Kingdom according to their light at that moment (vs. 35).

Simon and the Sinful Woman (7:36-50)

This story is a vivid illustration of the dual response mentioned in the preceding section. Simon is one of those who "rejected the purpose of God for themselves" (vs. 30), while the sinful woman is one of the "children" who vindicate God's wisdom in his method of working (vs. 35). This is one of three occasions, mentioned only by Luke, when Jesus dines with Pharisees (see 11:37; 14:1). Although Jesus kept company with outcasts, there is no evidence that he avoided the more privileged. Simon's motive in inviting him to dinner is not mentioned. The fact that the common courtesies were not extended to Jesus (vss. 44-46) has suggested to some that Simon invited him out of mere curiosity.

On this occasion a woman did what is often done in the Orient to this day, slipped in uninvited. She was a woman of evil reputation. The fact that she came prepared to anoint Jesus indicates that she had heard him preach and had already found forgiveness through him. The costly ointment she brought, and her acts of reverence and gratitude (vs. 38), were her thank offering for the new life she had found. When Simon saw that Jesus accepted all this, he could not believe that Jesus was even a prophet, for he did not seem to know what sort of woman this was. Jesus' reply, however, showed Simon that he knew what sort of man *he* was.

With a simple story, designed to show that love grows out of forgiveness, Jesus led Simon to confess the principle that the greater the forgiveness, the greater the love (vss. 41-43). Then he applied it straightforwardly. If one knows the depth of his own sin and the greatness of God's forgiveness, he cannot but love as this woman did. Those who, like the elder brother in the parable of the Prodigal, feel that by their own efforts they have earned the right to the Father's presence, never come into freedom and joy. Their faith is a cold, calculated, impersonal relationship. But the prodigals, who know they are not "worthy," who deserve only condemnation, and who yet find a forgiving welcome from the Father (15:11-24), are those whose love runs deep. It is they whose "sins are forgiven" and remain so, as the form of the Greek verb suggests (vs. 48). Faith, not works, is the basis of their salvation (vs. 50). And faith which accepts God's unmerited forgiveness in Christ issues in a love for him of which the highest human loves are but a pale reflection.

Right Hearing (8:1-21)

At this stage, Jesus had become more and more an itinerant preacher, going from place to place with "the good news of the kingdom," and followed by great crowds (vs. 1). It is a unique feature of Jesus' ministry that he raised womanhood from a position of servitude to men and social custom, giving women a place in his fellowship and service (vss. 2-3). The wealth of some of them supported Jesus and his disciples (vs. 3).

Jesus made a new departure in method at this point. He began to teach largely in parables. A parable is something intended to throw light on something else. It tells a story which in itself means one thing, but really points to something beyond itself. Only those understand it who see that to which it points. Why

did Jesus now begin to speak in parables? A ready answer would
be: To make truth plain. His own explanation, however, indicates that this answer will not do. In fact, it looks as though his
purpose were to veil truth (vs. 10). But would Jesus ever deliberately seek to keep the truth from men? The fact is, Jesus
used parables *both* to reveal and to conceal truth. Whether truth
was made plain or was hidden depended solely on the quality of
spiritual curiosity and receptivity of the hearer!

The situation in which Jesus began to use parables, and the
meaning of the first parable used, must be kept clearly in mind.
Luke indicates many times that during this period of Jesus' ministry, he was besieged by crowds (7:9, 11, 17, 24; 8:4, 19, 40,
45). Reports of him had spread through the whole of "the surrounding country" (7:17). Consequently, at the very time when
he began to teach in parables, "a great crowd came together and
people from town after town came to him" (8:4). Had Jesus'
purpose been merely to win a popular following, success would
have been his. But his purpose was to lead men to see that he
had brought the Kingdom of God, and to accept his summons
to enter it. In a sense, therefore, Jesus was defeated by his very
success, for his popularity at that moment was obscuring the real
issue. Furthermore, the time was growing short. John was already
in prison and was soon to be executed (Mark 6:17-29). Jesus
knew that a like fate awaited him. How could the crowds be
sifted? How could mere curiosity seekers, or those motivated
purely by self-interest, with no understanding or intention of true
discipleship, be separated from those of serious intent?

This could be done by parables. By those who had no ears to
hear, the story could be shrugged off. To those whose ears were
sensitive to higher truth, it would suggest a deeper meaning about
which they could think further, and about which they could, at
least, ask for an explanation (vss. 9-10). The hearer determines
the specific purpose of a parable for himself. Therefore, said
Jesus at the end of his first parable, if you have ears, use them!
(vs. 8).

The point to the parable of the Four Soils reinforces this. It is
a parable on right hearing. The four soils are all types of response to truth. All involve those who have *heard*. The seed is
God's Word—his setting forth of his deepest thoughts and inten-
tions toward men. This word falls with equal force on all human
hearts. Some are so hardened that there is no response (vs. 12).

Others are superficial, and do not endure (vs. 13). Still others are double-minded, allowing the affairs of this world to choke out their interest in the unseen world (vs. 14). But there are those who hear aright. They receive God's Word into the soil of their hearts and let it grow to maturity (vs. 15).

What is involved in their right hearing? Basically, it is to receive the Word with *faith*—to believe that Jesus has brought the Kingdom of God (vs. 12). This is the beginning. But the seed must be held fast in the heart to germinate, and must be cultivated with patience, to bear fruit (vs. 15). This leads to witnessing (vss. 16-18), and to obedient service (vss. 19-21).

To make one's faith a secret which never comes to light would be as self-contradictory as to light a lamp in order to cover it. The "secrets of the kingdom" (vs. 10) are secrets not because they are not announced, but because those who hear them often refuse to listen. Christianity is an open, a confessed faith. One must, therefore, take heed that he hears aright, for this makes him capable of hearing more, and thus of becoming a better witness. Careless hearing and poor witnessing lead to a degenerative process whereby one loses "even what he thinks that he has" (vs 18). For the way to maintain a right relationship to Jesus is to obey what is heard (vs. 21). There are no special privileges of kinship. All who "hear the word of God and do it" are brothers to the Son of man.

Right Hearing Illustrated (8:22-56)

Four miracles are here brought together. They illustrate Jesus' Lordship over nature, demons, disease, and death. Their location in the Gospel, however, and certain features which bind them into a unity, indicate that they have a special relation both to the materials which have gone before, and to the purpose of the whole section (6:12—9:51). Luke has earlier illustrated Jesus' Lordship over all the realms here presented (4:31—5:26; 7:11-17). Here these play a special role. The earlier part of this chapter has dealt with teaching about right hearing. The events here illustrate right hearing. In three of them, *faith* is mentioned as the right response (vss. 25, 48, 50). To hear Jesus' word aright is to connect it with his Person, and to believe it because one believes him. The response of the Gerasene people is an example of how not to hear (vs. 37). By contrast, the *obedience* of the man healed, even though Jesus' command ran counter to his own desire, suggests another aspect of right hearing (vs. 39).

Another feature common to all four events which does not stand out prominently, but is nonetheless of extreme importance in the light of the coming Great Confession (9:20), is the centrality of the disciples. It is they who are with him in the storm, and respond with fear and wonder (vs. 25). They are with him, too, in the land of the Gerasenes (vs. 26), observing, listening, pondering. In connection with the healing of the diseased woman, Peter is singled out for attention with one of his characteristic efforts to correct Jesus (vs. 45). It is Peter, John, and James who are taken into the room where Jairus' daughter is raised (vs. 51). In thus singling out the disciples, Luke intends to suggest that these events had a tremendous influence in leading them to the faith expressed in the Great Confession (9:20).

Luke does not indicate it, but the purpose of Jesus' crossing the lake was to get some rest from the pressure of the crowds who thronged him continually, and led him to near exhaustion (see Matt. 8:18; Mark 4:35-38). As soon as they sailed "he fell asleep" (vs. 23). The Lake of Galilee, around 700 feet below sea level, is cupped between hills which are "furrowed with ravines." Changes of temperature produce violent winds which rush through these ravines, causing sudden dangerous squalls (vss. 23-24). Jesus' stilling of the storm was a Messianic act. Where else could such a wonder be told so simply, with such dignity and reserve? It is not designed to awaken faith by a marvel but to deepen the faith of those who have already believed.

Jesus here shows his divine power. Lordship over nature, which is clearly attributed to God alone, is manifested by Jesus. More than that, in Jesus' day the peril of the sea's raging in storms was commonly attributed to demonic forces. The stilling of the waves, therefore, was another manifestation of Jesus' Lordship over the demonic. Jesus' rebuke of the disciples' lack of faith (vs. 25) indicates that they should already have known his Lordship over nature and over demons (see 5:1-11). Out of the experience, however, their faith was quickened, for their fear of the storm gave way to the fear which is produced by a sense of the divine Presence (vs. 25). And their suspicion deepened that One who could manifest God's power in this fashion was more than an ordinary man. The Great Confession is not far off!

No sooner did the group arrive at the opposite shore than Jesus was confronted by a demonic challenge (vss. 26-27). This was likely in Gentile territory, where Jesus had gone in the hope of rest. Even so, he would not refuse to meet the needs of one so torn by Satan. As was seen before (4:31-44), the presence of Jesus caused "torment" to the possessed, for Jesus and the demonic are in conflict, and Jesus is victor (vss. 28-29). "Legion" signifies the terrible plight of this victim (vs. 30).

The request of the demons not to be cast into the "abyss," and Jesus' permission for them to enter the swine, faces us with problems to which there is no clear answer. We can neither prove nor deny that evil spirits may act on beasts. Without evidence to deny it, it is best to accept the record here. Perhaps the uncontrolled terror of the swine indicates something of the dreadful plight of the man who was victimized by such destructive forces. As to why Jesus allowed the demons to destroy the swine which were the property of others, we again move in the realm of shadows. It may have been to give the victim some visible reassurance of his release from demonic bondage. This is, however, not a unique problem. It is merely a part of the larger problem of why God permits many manifestations of evil which seem unjust.

If God is Lord of nature, why does he not overrule its viciousness? The Bible hints that nature is cursed because of man's sin (see Gen. 3:17), and that it is included in the final redemption (see Rom. 8:19-23; Isa. 11:6-9; 65:17; II Peter 3:13; Rev. 21:1). Just as in the stilling of the storm Jesus manifested his Lordship over the disorder of nature, yet reserved his final victory over it until the end, so here he manifests his Lordship over the demonic, yet reserves his destruction of demonic powers to the end. Matthew reports the demons as saying: "Have you come here to torment us *before the time?*" (Matt. 8:29). That is the time of the final destruction. Why Jesus ruled the demons, and yet permitted them to continue their existence even in swine, is only part of a much larger problem. Reverent hesitancy at this point is preferable to faulty solutions or brash denials.

The response of the Gerasene people (vss. 34-37) is an eloquent revelation of the sin of our own hearts. They could not deny the saving effect of Jesus on their formerly wretched neighbor. But One who produced such results in such a disturbing way was One with whom they preferred to have nothing to do. Jesus always disturbs complacency, even demands the sacrifice of material goods, that his saving work may be done. Since his presence is so dangerous, it is easier to ask him to leave.

Jesus left at their request, but they could not be rid of him
so easily. His own work was largely confined to "the lost sheep
of the house of Israel" (Matt. 15:24). But he left behind him
in this pagan territory a witness, through whose testimony the
people would still have to reckon with him. Jesus' Lordship was
not confined to Israel. He was Lord of the Gentile world as well.
It was quite natural that the man who had been so marvelously
delivered should want to stay near Jesus. Perhaps he feared that
the demons would return and victimize him again. And if Jesus
were not there—? The safeguard against this was to be at work
for his Lord (vs. 39). Unless faith issues in obedient action it is
no permanent safeguard against evil (see Luke 11:24-26).

Jesus returned to crowds and a request for healing (vss.
40-42). The request was desperate, for the child "was dying"
(vs. 42). The interweaving of the story of the healing of the
diseased woman (vss. 43-48) with that of Jairus' daughter, however, indicates the sovereign certainty of Jesus. He was not pan-
icked into haste. With regard to his ability to help, it makes little
difference whether the child was "dying" or "dead."

How Jesus was conscious of the power that had gone forth
from him, we cannot know. He may have seen the woman's act,
unknown to her, then made her volunteer the information for
her good. On the other hand, he may have felt power going from
him without seeing her act. His purpose in bringing the healing
of the woman to light, even over the protest of Peter (vs. 45),
lay in the fact that her healing was not as important as her personal relation to him. She seems to have had a rather magical
idea that a touch of his garment was all that was needed to restore
her to health. And this it did! But Jesus wanted to lead her to a
faith which rested in personal acquaintance and open confession
of him. Then she could go with a deeper "peace" than that which
mere recovery of health could bring (vs. 48).

Jesus' arrival at the home of Jairus confronted him once more
with the terrible lordship of death over human life (see 7:11-17
and discussion there). The news of the child's death suggests the
finality of man's submission to it (vs. 49). She is dead. It is too
late. And when death says his last word, man is dumb. And how
senseless death is! She was only twelve years old (vs. 42). And
an only child! But senseless or not, death is master. And when
Jesus suggests that the child might be awakened from death's
slumber, he is ridiculed (vs. 53). Putting out all curiosity seekers,

taking only the parents and three of his most intimate disciples, Jesus entered the death chamber, and turned death into life (vss. 54-55).

The Apostolic Mission and Herod's Question (9:1-9)

Two things lay behind Jesus' sending out of the Twelve. For one thing, the time of his own ministry was short. One could not stir up the multitudes as Jesus had done without soon running afoul of the authorities. John's experience had shown that. In order, therefore, to make his announcement of the Kingdom as widespread as possible in the shortest time, Jesus commissioned and empowered his Apostles to go forth in his name. The second reason for their commission was that they should begin preparation for the work they must take over after Jesus' death. Some experience of work in his name during his lifetime was necessary before they could carry on alone following the Resurrection.

The instructions given were not for their permanent work, but only for this hurried mission. They were to take no provisions, but to live on the generosity of those to whom they went (vs. 3). They were to be content with their lot, not moving about from house to house to seek better entertainment (vs. 4). They were not to press their message. It was an announcement of the Kingdom's presence. If men would not believe it, they were to shake off the dust from their feet—an oriental gesture of dissociation and judgment—and go elsewhere (vs. 5). The aim was to take the "good news" as far as possible in the time allowed.

This widespread activity stirred Herod Antipas to attention (vs. 7). He had surely heard of Jesus' activity before this. But the movement could no longer be ignored. The people were suggesting that Jesus was one of the old prophets returned, or Elijah promised by Malachi (Mal. 4:5), or even John the Baptist raised from the dead (vss. 7-8). Herod had beheaded John. He thought he had thereby rid his kingdom of Messianic troubles. But here they were again. "Who is this about whom I hear such things?" he asked (vs. 9). And he sought to see Jesus. That privilege was not granted him until the day of Jesus' death (23:6-12). His behavior at that time indicates that his desire had no good purpose.

The Feeding of the Five Thousand (9:10-17)

The withdrawal to Bethsaida upon the return of the Twelve was perhaps to seek quiet for rest and further instruction. An even stronger motive, however, was to escape Herod, who was now seeking to see him. Bethsaida was outside Herod's territory. It could not be that Jesus should "perish away from Jerusalem" (13:33). Hence, he must avoid falling into Herod's hands as John had, and thus meeting his fate prematurely.

Mark tells us that Jesus' withdrawal was by boat, and that the crowds went by foot around the lake to be on hand when he and the Twelve arrived (Mark 6:30-33). The leisure Jesus sought he could not find. Yet he welcomed the crowds and continued his work of announcing the Kingdom and healing (vs. 11). The feeding of the multitudes is the only miracle recorded in all four Gospels. There is no doubt that the disciples looked upon it as of extreme importance. Wherein did its meaning lie?

It, of course, suggests that Jesus is concerned about the physical needs of men. Although he would not make bread for himself, and would not use miracles to gain a following (4:3-4), yet on this occasion he demonstrated his concern for legitimate physical necessities. From this the Church learns its obligation to minister as it may to human hunger and need in all its forms (Gal. 6:10). But Luke connects this miracle directly with the disciples' confession of Jesus' Messiahship. John does the same thing (6:66-71), and Matthew seems to see some vital connection between the two (16:5-20). What is the relationship?

The clue lies in the fact that the Jews thought of the coming of the Messiah under the picture of a Messianic banquet. Jesus himself spoke of sitting "at table in the kingdom of God" (13:29). When another mentioned the blessedness of eating bread in the Kingdom of God, Jesus told the parable of the "great banquet" (14:15-24). One of the Old Testament passages about the Servant of the Lord spoke of the "day of salvation" as a time when God's people should "not hunger" (Isa. 49:8, 10; see also Rev. 7:16). The feeding of the five thousand, then, is an enacted parable announcing the arrival of the Messianic Age. They had already been fed at the hands of Messiah. They had had a foretaste of the coming Messianic banquet. The people, however, were concerned only with the stilling of their hunger, and did not read the deep meaning of this (see John 6:26-27). The coming confession of the disciples (Luke 9:20) suggests that they had seen in the miracle a *sign* of a deeper reality.

The Great Confession (9:18-27)

Jesus' announcement of the Kingdom had been made in Galilee. Herod was becoming restive over him (9:7-9), and all signs
pointed to the fact that a fate similar to that of John awaited
him. Hence he withdrew to the north, clear out of Herod's realm,
to Caesarea Philippi (Mark 8:27). But he must finally go to
Jerusalem to proclaim himself there as the bringer of God's
Kingdom. There at the center of the Old Israel he must meet
his fate. The question now is whether the Twelve have come to
any real understanding of him, beyond that of the masses. Is
there a nucleus of the New Israel prepared to follow him to Jerusalem, to see his final rejection by the Old Israel, and yet come
through it as permanent witnesses to him? In other words, is
there a germ of life in the New Israel which, however weak it
may be, is vital? The importance of this question may be seen in
the fact that Jesus withdrew from the multitudes to be alone with
the Twelve, to prepare for this critical moment in prayer (vs. 18).

Jesus had not openly declared himself as Messiah. The demons
had witnessed to him (4:41; 8:28), and he had claimed that in
himself the signs of the Messianic Age were fulfilled (7:22). His
works, too, as we have seen, were indirect testimonies to his
Messianic significance. But, true to his decision at the Temptation (4:1-13; see discussion), he had taken no measures to proclaim himself openly, either by wonders or by force. Knowledge
of his true nature must rest on faith, and faith alone. Hence, Jesus
draws from the disciples their confession, rather than putting it
into their mouth.

Peter's confession shows that the disciples had seen in Jesus
more than the masses had seen (vs. 20; see also vss. 7, 8, 19).
The living germ was there. There was the nucleus of a New Israel, who had heard the voice of God and had seen his redemptive action in Jesus. Although Jesus would be rejected by the
Old Israel, he did have a people—the true people of God—who
had responded to his call to repent and to enter the Kingdom he
had brought. As we shall see later, the disciples did not understand all that their confession meant. They had much yet to
learn. And there would be a moment when the germ of the New
Israel would be so deeply buried under misunderstanding, sorrow, and disillusionment, that it appeared to be completely killed
(22:54—23:49; Matt. 26:56). But on Easter morning it broke

through the sod again. The New Israel became a community witnessing to their faith (24:48; Acts 1:8).

Until then, the disciples were to keep silence about their confession (vs. 21). It involved something quite other than they thought. Like a bombshell exploding in their midst, Jesus for the first time announced that he must suffer, and on the third day be raised (vs. 22). He was Messiah, as they had confessed, but he must now reinterpret their conceptions of Messiahship. The Messiah was to fulfill his mission by suffering. He was to reign by the power of sacrificial love. He was to be authenticated as Messiah by God through a resurrection after death. In his announcement of suffering Jesus therefore changed their word "Messiah" into "Son of man," a term which did not have all the mistaken political implications of the word "Messiah" (vs. 22; see also 5:24 and discussion). All this the disciples could not at this time understand. More than once Jesus told them, but it was meaningless (9:44-45; 17:25; 18:31-34). Only after his death, and after God's vindication of him in the Resurrection, could he explain it to them in all its fullness of meaning (24:25-27, 44-49). Then, after God had proclaimed him Messiah in the true sense, they were to placard it publicly to the ends of the earth (Acts 2:14-36). Until then they were to be silent.

But not only was Jesus to suffer. His people, too, must follow in his steps (vss. 23-26). One must "deny" himself. This is the same word used to describe Peter's denial later. As Peter disclaimed any relationship to Jesus, each follower must decisively renounce all obligations to the old self, and "put on the new nature, created after the likeness of God" in Jesus Christ (Eph. 4:24). This self-renunciation is accomplished through taking up the cross. The figure is taken from the Roman custom of having a condemned person carry his own cross to the place of execution, a custom which the Galileans knew only too well. To take up one's cross, then, is *voluntarily* to lift to one's shoulders the instrument of his own execution, and to follow Christ to the death. Paul put it clearly: "I have been crucified with Christ" (Gal. 2:20). This is a "daily" process, a progressive and continuous crucifixion of one's natural self-centeredness (vs. 23). This involves sharing the humiliation of Christ, that we may also share his glory when his Kingdom comes in its fullness (vs. 26).

The meaning of verse 27 is impossible to determine with any finality. It has been variously referred to the Transfiguration, the

Resurrection and Ascension, Pentecost, the spread of Christianity, the growth of Christian theology, the destruction of Jerusalem in A.D. 70, and the Second Coming. The fact that only *some* to whom Jesus spoke would be living seems to rule out the first three of these. The spread of the Church, the growth of Christian theology, and the destruction of Jerusalem might fill the time requirements, but they were hardly the coming of the Kingdom of God, only signs of it. That Jesus meant his Second Coming seems ruled out by the fact that he refused to make any predictions as to its date (Mark 13:32; Acts 1:7). It is perhaps best to admit that we do not know what it means.

The Transfiguration (9:28-43a)

At least three attitudes toward this event are possible. One is to explain it away—which has often been done—as merely a symbolic story without historic reality. A second is to try to explain it by some combination of natural factors, such as hazy sunlight through morning clouds and the suggestiveness of the half-conscious state between waking and sleeping. The third is to confess a mystery which we do not understand, but before which we worship. The mystery took place in prayer (vs. 29). It is best understood in prayer. The appearance of Jesus here can be likened only to that of his resurrection body, which was both like and unlike his normal appearance (24:36-43; John 20:1—21:23). Something of the glory of the world of his Father, which he had left to take the form of a Servant, momentarily broke through, and the three disciples who were with him had a foretaste of the post-Resurrection appearances (vs. 28).

The significance of the Transfiguration was at least fourfold. First, it confirmed Jesus in his decision to go to Jerusalem to suffer, which he had but a few days earlier announced to his disciples (vs. 22). Second, it both confirms the disciples in their confession of his Messiahship (vs. 20), and commands them to accept Jesus' new teaching about his suffering. "Listen to him!" said the voice (vs. 35). Unreasonable as his announcement of his suffering may seem, and incongruous though it may be with your idea of Messiahship, nevertheless listen to what he is saying, and believe it! You are the ones who do not know what you are saying (vs. 33). Jesus does. Listen to him! Third, the appearance of Moses and Elijah, the founder and the reformer of the Old Israel, representing the Law and the Prophets, indicates that

Jesus is the fulfillment of all that they were anticipating (vss. 30-31). What the Law intended, and what the prophets promised, is now here in its fullness in Jesus. Fourth, the fact that Moses and Elijah were talking with Jesus about the "departure [literally, the "exodus"], which he was to accomplish at Jerusalem" (vs. 31), shows that the fulfillment of the plan of God is to come through the Cross. Jesus is shown to be God's eternal Son, not in spite of the Cross, but precisely *because* of it. The whole plan of God from the beginning was moving forward to this event. Jesus was the lamb "destined before the foundation of the world" (I Peter 1:19-20). The partial deliverance of his people wrought by God at the first Exodus is now to be completed in the new Exodus —the Crucifixion and the Resurrection.

The healing of the epileptic boy is definitely bound in with the Transfiguration. Raphael in his great painting of the Transfiguration has caught this connection by placing both scenes on one canvas. The scene of glory on the Mount reveals the wonder and beauty of God's world, where sin and death have no place. The scene of wretchedness below reveals the terribleness of the human plight, where man is subjected to evils with which he cannot cope. Had Christ, as Peter suggested (vs. 33), stayed on the Mount of glory, the scene below would have remained unchanged. He had to leave the height, descend once more into the valleys of human need, and confront again the unbelief and stupidity of his own followers (vss. 45-50), the forces of evil which had man in their power, the rejection of his people, the blindness of the religious leaders, the mockery of the powers of world empire. All this was brought to a focus in the Cross.

The One who at the Baptism (3:21-22) had chosen to identify himself with the sin of man, must carry this identification through to its logical consequence. "The Son of man *must* suffer" (vs. 22). To come directly from the Mount of Transfiguration to this tragic scene of unbelief and helplessness brought sharp pangs of suffering to Jesus, which must have been a prelude to the Cross. "How long am I to be with you?" (vs. 41) are words of one who is living in a foreign exile, far from his native habitat, and who is longing for the coming of the Kingdom, when his suffering will be over and his victory complete. The people were astonished at the divine majesty with which Jesus achieved what his disciples could not. But he immediately reminded his disciples that more is involved in his ministry than causing people to marvel at his mighty deeds (vs. 44). He must lay hold of the powers of evil in costly action to break their grip forever. Therefore, very shortly he will "set his face to go to Jerusalem" (vs. 51).

Weaknesses of the Disciples (9:43b-50)

The disciples had come a long way. They had surpassed the masses in their understanding of Jesus (vss. 18-20). They had confessed him as Messiah. How far they were, however, from understanding the nature of Jesus' Messiahship, Luke shows us with three brief pictures. A second time Jesus announced his suffering (vs. 44). The disciples, however, were so spiritually obtuse that it had no meaning (vs. 45). Suffering and Messiahship were so incompatible that they simply could not be put together in their thinking at that time. They were obsessed with other things (vss. 46-48).

When Jesus was preparing himself for his death, the disciples were quarreling over who should be greatest in the Kingdom (vs. 46). Here was self-centered ambition of the worst sort. Did the question arise partly because three of them had been favored on two occasions? (8:51; 9:28). Were the others jealous? Did the three boast of their privileges? In any case, Jesus had to remind them that in his Kingdom greatness did not consist in honors, but in service. And service not for reward, but in the name of Jesus (vs. 48). He is himself the example of true greatness.

The disciples' ambition led them to spiritual presumption and intolerance. Since they were especially used by Jesus, they objected to others working in Jesus' name who were not members of their group, even though the others were engaged in the worthy work of casting out demons (vs. 49). Jesus rebuked this spirit. Not to be with *Christ* is to be against him (11:23). But those who labor for Christ are for *us*, whether they work within the confines of our own group or not. Paul learned this from his Lord so fully that he rejoiced even when Christ was preached from false motives (Phil. 1:15-18; see also I Cor. 3:3-9).

Here ends Luke's record of Jesus' Galilean ministry. Jesus must now teach the disciples much about the Kingdom of the Suffering Servant (9:51—19:27), then complete his work by death and resurrection.

MESSIAH MOVES TOWARD JERUSALEM:
THE KINGDOM OF THE SERVANT
Luke 9:51—19:27

The first section of the Gospel was climaxed by Jesus' reinterpretation of his Messiahship in terms of the Suffering Servant (9:18-22). The second is introduced by his determined departure for Jerusalem to suffer (9:51). Although Luke keeps reminding the reader that Jesus is on the way to Jerusalem (9:51, 53; 13:22, 33; 17:11; 18:31; 19:11, 28), the length of time and the amount of material which intervene seem to suggest that this is not the report of one direct, continuous journey. The geographical information is very indistinct. The materials seem to be quite independent of place and time. The mention of Jerusalem is as much theological as geographical. Luke means that from now on, what is to happen at Jerusalem dominates everything that Jesus says and does. The shadow of the Cross falls on this whole section. Luke takes opportunity to insert a large block of materials which are not given in the other Gospels (9:51—18:14 is nearly all unique). Most of these are teachings about the Kingdom. As the conceptions of the Messiah in Jesus' day were radically reinterpreted by him, so were the current ideas of the Kingdom of God. This section, therefore, largely deals with Jesus' teachings on the Kingdom in the light of the Suffering Servant who was its King.

Servants of the Kingdom (9:51—10:24)

It is significant that the first incident in Jesus' journey to Jerusalem was a repetition of the Temptation (4:1-13), and of his rejection by men (4:16-30). This shows immediately what "the days . . . for him to be received up" held: rejection, suffering, death (vs. 51). His decision to go to Jerusalem, then, was not that of a tourist. It was a steadfast decision to do the will of his Father (vss. 51-53). How far the disciples were from understanding Jesus and his Kingdom is shown by their desire to call down fire from heaven to consume those who rejected him (vs. 54). Were these not the hated Samaritans, who were under God's judgment anyway? And had not Elijah dealt summarily with those who opposed God's will? (II Kings 1:10-12). The fact that Jesus "rebuked" his disciples (vs. 55), as he had re-

buked demons (4:35; 8:24; 9:42), suggests how he sensed in
this the temptation of the Evil One. His disciples would have to
learn that to follow the Suffering Servant, they must *love even
their enemies* (6:27; 23:34).

The story of the three candidates for discipleship brings together incidents which may have taken place at different times
(vss. 57-62; see also Matt. 8:19-22). They are grouped here by
affinity of subject matter. The first man was acting on the basis
of emotional enthusiasm (vs. 57). Jesus repeatedly sought to
warn men against the peril of action based on mere feeling (11:
27-28; 22:33-34). One must count the cost and be ready to share
Jesus' privation (vs. 58). This means the abandonment of all
security except that of commitment to God. The answer of Jesus
to the request of the second seems harsh (vss. 59-60). Certainly
Jesus was not denying the claims of family loyalties (18:20;
Matt. 15:3-6). He was saying, however, that when there is a
conflict of loyalties, those of the Kingdom take precedence over
all others, no matter how sacred. Not to be overlooked, too, is
the fact that Jesus is going to his death in order to destroy the
power of death. The spiritually dead, therefore, may mourn the
dead, but those who follow Christ are to proclaim the good news
of life in him (vs. 60). Jesus' answer to the third, in the form of a
proverb (vs. 62), indicates that this man's resolution was weak.
As a plowman who does not keep his eye constantly on the
goal toward which he moves cannot plow a straight furrow, so
he who is mindful of the old associations cannot do adequate
service in the Kingdom. There is even danger that a lingering
look on the old loyalties could so weaken one's resolution that he
would surrender the claims of the Kingdom.

The close relationship between the sending of the seventy (10:
1-12) and Jesus' journey into Samaria and Perea, suggests that
this was a dramatic way to emphasize the universality of his mission. The Jews considered 70 to be the number of the Gentile
nations. Although Jesus' own work was largely confined to the
Jews (Matt. 15:24), there are clear indications that, quickened
by the Old Testament promises (Isa. 42:6; 49:6), he intended
his followers to take the gospel to all men (10:33-37; 13:28-30;
14:23; 20:16; Matt. 15:22-28; 20:16; 21:43). The instruction to
pray for workers in the harvest indicates two things: first, prayer
is a part of God's plan for achieving what he wants done in the
world; second, the harvest is God's, not ours. His word is the

seed. He produces growth. All we do is to help in reaping (10:2).

The instructions were for the temporary, hurried mission of preparing his way at that time, and they can be applied permanently only in principle. Witnesses of the Kingdom are always in a hostile environment, but are to win their way by meekness, not by force (10:3). The haste of the temporary mission made it imperative that they not take the time which oriental greetings demanded, and that they not burden themselves with provisions (vs. 4). In contrast to the Zealots to whom "revolution" was the watchword, their greeting was to be one of "peace" (vs. 5). If their greeting was received, well; if not, they were to go elsewhere (vs. 6). They were worthy of their keep, but should be content with whatever they were given (vs. 7). Healing and proclamation of the nearness of the Kingdom would be their work in each town (vss. 8-9). If their ministry was refused, they were to dramatize God's judgment on that town (vss. 10-11). Because the privilege of the inhabitants was greater, the judgment would be worse than that of Sodom (vs. 12). Chorazin, Bethsaida, and Capernaum had already rejected Jesus and failed to see the meaning of his mighty works (vs. 13). Their pride of position with God would be greatly humbled when, in the Judgment, the pagans escaped with lighter consequences than they (vss. 14-15). To reject Christ's representatives is to reject Christ, and to reject Christ is to reject God (vs. 16). The disciples' task, therefore, is both glorious and dreadful.

The return of the seventy to Jesus is the occasion for one of the most exalted experiences in his entire career. In his name, demons had been conquered (vs. 17). In this, Jesus saw a promise of the whole ministry of his Church, through which the proclamation of his coming victory over Satan would be carried to the ends of the earth. With an authority given by Jesus, the Church would have power which its enemies could not finally destroy (vss. 18-19). Serpents and scorpions are symbols of spiritual enemies, and are not to be taken literally. Although the Church may rightly rejoice in her achievements through the power of Christ, there is something greater over which to joy— the mercy of God through whom men find salvation (vs. 20; see Exod. 32:32; Isa. 4:3; Heb. 12:23; Rev. 3:5; 20:15).

The vision of Satan's fall lifted Jesus, in the Holy Spirit, into an ecstasy of joy (vs. 21). He burst out in a prayer of thanksgiving for the fact that although those who considered them-

selves wise in religious affairs—particularly the learned scribes—
had failed to understand the meaning of his coming, there were
simple-hearted people to whom this had been revealed. Faith is
the simple response of the whole heart to what God has done in
Christ. This is confirmed by the statement in verse 22. There is a
mystery about the Person of Christ known only to God. Therefore, because of this intimate relation between Jesus and God,
Jesus can make God known to men. This he does to all who accept him, and this is the glorious goal toward which all of God's
working in history had been directed (vss. 23-24).

Characteristics of the Kingdom (10:25—12:59)

At this point Luke introduces a series of teachings which may
be arranged under the general theme of qualities, or character-
istics, of the Kingdom. They embody both direct teaching and
parable, and occasionally center around an incident.

Limitless Love (10:25-37)

What must one do to reach eternal blessedness? (vs. 25). Out
of this question posed by a doctor of the Law came the parable
of the Good Samaritan. What do you find in the Old Testament,
Jesus asked (vs. 26). The "newness" in Jesus' teaching was not
a new Law, but the insistence on finding the will of God which
stands behind the old commandments. The lawyer replied with
a summary of the Old Testament Law common among the rabbis
which Jesus strongly approved (Mark 12:28-34)—love to God,
expressed in love to one's neighbor (Luke 10:27; Deut. 6:5; Lev.
19:18). After commending his answer, Jesus said simply: "Do
this [continually], and you will live" (vs. 28).

The lawyer, desiring to justify his question which Jesus had
answered so simply, insisted that there was more to it than that.
If I am to manifest love to God in my dealings with my neighbor, I must first determine who my neighbor is (vs. 29). The
lawyer thus suggests limits to love. There must be those to whom
the obligation to love does not apply. This was an effort to evade
the real issue by theoretical discussion. Furthermore, it focused
attention on the worthiness of the object of love rather than on
the condition of heart of the one who is to do the loving. The
priest and the Levite, journeying back to their home after per-
forming their Temple duties in Jerusalem (vss. 31-32), could have

argued this question at length and with great skill. A Samaritan, however, who was considered heretical and whose theological judgment would have had no worth to the lawyer, did not theorize, but acted (vss. 33-35). He not only met the emergency needs which compassion might have suggested, but intelligently concerned himself with the complete restoration of the victim.

At this point, Jesus threw back the question to the lawyer, but in a different form (vs. 36). Not, Who *was* the neighbor? but, Who *acted* like a neighbor? The question is not, Who is worthy of my love? It is, rather, Have I the kind of love which seeks the good of all men under all circumstances? Love is not a self-centered feeling of achievement according to a predetermined standard of obligation. It is rather the spontaneous overflow of a heart that forgets itself in the presence of any human need. As is true of Jesus' teaching throughout, there is more involved here than mere ethical instruction. No man can perfectly fulfill the demands of love. Jesus alone has done it. He was what Luther called God's Good Samaritan for all men. The story here is a record of his own action. It can be approximated in us only as he dwells in us, and gives us the gift of his own compassion. The record does not tell us the outcome in the life of the scribe. It rather directs Jesus' words to the reader: "Go and do likewise" (vs. 37).

Communion with God (10:38-42)

The close relation of the story of Mary and Martha to that of the Good Samaritan supplements the teaching there set forth. Service in the name of love may degenerate into mere human activity empty of eternal value, if it is divorced from constant communion with the One who is the source of all good. Martha's motives were high. Jesus was her guest, and she wished to do him honor. But she sought to honor him with service and material gifts rather than with spiritual communion. As a result, she became "distracted," or "drawn about in different directions" (vs. 40). This led to inner anxiety and external bustling (vs. 41), occasioned not by necessity but by her own sense of values. She created her own problem by placing too much value on things which are transitory, and too little on that "good portion" which cannot be taken away—fellowship with God in Jesus (vs. 42). In Jesus' gentle dealing with Martha, he repeats in different form the issue on which he had stood at the Temptation: "Man shall

not live by bread alone" (4:4), an issue which appears frequently in Luke's Gospel (12:16-21; 16:19-31). Activity and
service are necessary. But when they become the source of dis-
traction and anxiety and bustling, the cure is to sit at the feet of
Jesus and listen. Worship is as important as service, and service
has Christian meaning only when it is rooted in worship.

Prayer (11:1-13)

How naturally the foregoing leads to the thought of prayer!
Jesus' response to a request to teach his disciples to pray "as
John taught his disciples" (11:1), suggests again the close relationship between the work of John and of Jesus. The fact that
the Church preserved variant forms of this prayer (vss. 2-4; Matt.
6:9-13) indicates that it was given not to be used as an exclusive
formula for prayer, but as a guide.

The familiar address to God, "Father," does not take its meaning from faulty human fatherhood (vs. 2). Its meaning lies
rather in all that Jesus revealed of God in his relationship as the
Son (10:22), and can be rightly used by us only as we come to
God through him (John 14:13-14; 15:7; 16:23-24). Two requests are offered with regard to God: first, that his name be
hallowed; that is, that the chants of the heavenly beings over the
holiness of God be echoed by men (Isa. 6:3; Rev. 4:8). Second,
that the Kingdom brought into being by Jesus come in its fullness (see Luke 10:2). Three requests relate to believers (vss. 3-4):
first, for physical provision a day at a time; second, for forgiveness, which cannot be merited but can be ours only as we are
willing to forgive men's lesser debts to us (Matt. 18:23-35); and
third, that God garrison our weakness in temptation (22:31-32).

Encouragement to prayer is given in two brief parables. The
first, that of the Importunate Friend, has to do with the spirit of
urgency which should lie behind our praying (vss. 5-10). This
is not to suggest that God is one whose reluctance to give must
be overcome. It may, however, imply that although God is desirous of answering our prayers, he cannot do it lightly nor
cheaply in response to half-hearted desire on our part. *The im-
portunity is necessary for us, not God.* The second encourages
us to believe that prayer is heard by God (vss. 11-13). It argues
from the lesser to the greater. If human parents, faulty and sinful,
will not deceive their children by giving them harmful things instead of fulfilling their real needs, how much more will God, who

is wholly good, answer our prayers aright. The "Holy Spirit" is
the all-inclusive gift, God's gift of himself (vs. 13).

Spiritual Discernment (11:14-36)

An attack on Jesus led him to speak of the spiritual discernment which is necessary in order to recognize the Kingdom in
him. The casting out of a demon from a dumb man led to the
charge that Jesus did his work by the power of Satan (vs. 15).
Jesus' reply indicated first the foolishness of such a charge. Satan
is the one who binds men, not frees them (13:16). Would he,
therefore, work against himself? (vss. 17-18). Furthermore, why
do they blame in him what they praise in their own sons? (vs.
19). Whether their sons were successful is unimportant. At least,
they were praised for trying to do what Jesus did! If, therefore,
the charge that he did his work by the power of Satan was absurd, the only possible explanation was that he did it "by the
finger of God" (vs. 20; see Exod. 8:19; 31:18; Ps. 8:3). A spiritually discerning person would reach this conclusion, facing the
"if" of verse 20 with the evidence of Jesus' works. Satan was
strong, as his hold on those such as the dumb man suggested.
But Jesus was the "one stronger than he" who snatched away his
armor and delivered his victims (vss. 21-22). In this conflict,
neutrality is impossible (vs. 23).

A warning is given to those who lack the spiritual discernment to see that Jesus, in overthrowing the work of Satan in
men's lives (vss. 24-26), has brought the Kingdom. If they do not
recognize God's victory over evil in Jesus, they will be religiously
much worse off than they were before. The measure to which
Jesus has set their spiritual house in order exposes them to worse
assaults of Satan if they do not believe. Discernment of the
meaning of Jesus for men does not lie in any superficial, external approval of his teaching or his human personality. Personal compliments are not in order! (vs. 27). To hear the word
of God from Jesus, and to respond in obedient action, is the
discernment which he desires (vs. 28). No other relationship to
him is important, not even that of his mother. This verse should
have sufficed to prevent Mariolatry in the Roman Church.

Genuine spiritual discernment is rooted in the inner disposition to repent and believe (vss. 29-32). In response to the demand for "a sign from heaven" (vs. 16), Jesus turned the
thoughts of his questioners inward to the condition of their own

hearts. His miracles were signs, if they had had the spiritual insight rightly to interpret them. No special heavenly sign, no sensational heavenly wonder, which they could accept without the necessity of faith, would be given. Jesus had determined this at the Temptation (4:9-12). There is always a risk in faith. Whether one takes it or not depends on the quality of his inner life more than on convincing wonders. Jesus himself is the final wonder. Repentance and belief on him are the means of recognizing that he has brought the Kingdom. For those who finally refuse him, he will come as Judge. In the Judgment the pagans, who were impressed with the wisdom of Solomon and repented at the preaching of Jonah (vss. 30-32), will judge the men of Jesus' generation, who failed to discern in him something far greater—the One who is "the power of God and the wisdom of God" (I Cor. 1:24). Verses 33-36 are a continuation of what Jesus has been saying. He is God's "light," set forth for all to see (vs. 33). But as light is useless to a blind man, whose whole body moves in darkness because his eye is bad, so their spiritual blindness has kept them from seeing him (vss. 34-35). If their spiritual sight, however, admits the light of Christ, they will live entirely in the light (vs. 36). It is their blindness, not lack of evidence, which makes them demand a "sign from heaven" (vs. 16).

Reality (11:37—12:3)

An invitation to a meal with a Pharisee gave Jesus opportunity to contrast the religious reality of his Kingdom with religious formalism and hypocrisy. Jesus startled his host by neglecting to wash his hands before eating (vss. 37-38). The handwashing had nothing to do with hygienic cleanliness, but was a Pharisaic prescription to remove the moral uncleanness they felt was acquired by contact with unholy people and things. It had grown out of tradition, and was not prescribed by the Law. It was one of many indications that official piety had degenerated into concern with appearances, rather than with reality. Hence, Jesus upbraided this concern with the ceremonial cleansing of externals when the inner life was wicked (vs. 39). The God who made the material universe also made the inner life of man. To serve him means to keep one's heart clean (vs. 40). And the best evidence of a true heart toward God is to share one's goods with a needy neighbor. This will cleanse the life more than concern with religious ceremonies (vs. 41).

A series of six woes follows. The tithe was intended as an acknowledgment of God's provision and an offering of love. Woe on a religion which had become a substitute for justice and the love of God—a means of escaping the full demands of obedience to God by the scrupulous fulfillment of a part of the letter of the law (vs. 42; Micah 6:8). Woe on a religion which had become a means of enhancing the vanity of men rather than the glory of God (vs. 43). To step on a grave was defiling to a Jew (Num. 19:16). Unidentified graves which might be touched without knowing it, therefore, were a menace. Woe, therefore, on a religion whose deceitfully beautiful exterior covered up the fact that the heart was dead (vs. 44). The lawyers (scribes) were particularly blameworthy, for in their hands lay the interpretation of the Law (vs. 45). Woe to them, for through their clever casuistry they had placed intolerable religious requirements on the people, but by the same means had contrived ways of escaping these themselves (vs. 46). Woe to them, for although they erected monuments to the prophets, by refusing obedience to the prophets' word and witness to Jesus they joined their fathers who had slain the prophets (vss. 47-51). Therefore, the cumulative judgment of the centuries will fall on them in the destruction of Jerusalem (21:32). Woe to them, for they had closed the door to the knowledge of God by misinterpreting the Scriptures, and had, so to speak, thrown the key away (vs. 52).

The discourse aroused the strong hostility of the Pharisees (vss. 53-54). A tremendous crowd of onlookers gathered, interested in this One who had the courage to attack the entrenched religious leadership. The incident closed with Jesus' warning that hypocrisy had no place in his Kingdom (12:1). The warning was reinforced by the reminder that at the Day of Judgment all the secrets of the heart will be publicly placarded before "the eyes of him with whom we have to do" (vss. 2-3; Heb. 4:13).

Courageous Witness (12:4-12)

The hostility aroused by Jesus' dealing with the Pharisees suggested the need for courage on the part of members of his Kingdom. Those who are "friends" of Jesus may even have to face death in their witness for him. They are not, however, to fear those who put them to death, for their judgment is temporary, and not final. It deals only with physical, not eternal, death (vs. 4). The only one to fear is God, the final Judge, in whose hands

eternal destinies lie (vs. 5; Isa. 8:12-15; I Peter 1:17; 3:14-15).
True fear of God, however, means not terror but trust. God is
One who is concerned about the smallest details of life, even the
death of sparrows (vs. 6). Nothing that happens to his children as
they witness for him, therefore—not even death—can take place
apart from his providential care, nor be meaningless (vs. 7).

Encouragement to witness lies in Jesus' identification of himself with his disciples. To confess Jesus before men, even though
it should bring condemnation before human judges, means that
he will confess us before God, the final Judge, who for his sake
will grant us acquittal (vs. 8). Jesus, however, can only witness
the truth before the heavenly Judge. If we deny our relationship
to him, he will be forced to deny that we were his disciples (vs.
9). The infinite patience and mercy of Jesus is to be seen in the
fact that he does not judge denials of him on the basis of personal affronts. The personal affront of rejection of him may be
forgiven (vs. 10; 23:34; I Tim. 1:13). The unforgivable blasphemy against the Holy Spirit is somehow related to ascribing
Jesus' works to demonic powers (11:15; Matt. 12:24-32). This
is more than a personal affront. It is a state of spiritual stupor
which confuses the Spirit of God with the Devil. The power to
receive grace may be lost. God alone, however, and not we, must
judge who has reached this stage. The friends of Jesus, who
have seen the Spirit of God at work in him, are to be free from
anxiety when they are called upon to witness in a hostile environment, for the Holy Spirit himself will teach them what to say
(vss. 11-12). This was literally fulfilled in the later experience of
the Church (Acts 4:13; 7:1-53; II Tim. 4:16-17).

Freedom from Materialism (12:13-34)

A request for Jesus to settle an inheritance dispute gave him
opportunity to deal with the insidious blight of "things" on men's
souls (vss. 13-15). In so doing, Jesus was not showing indifference to the claims of legal justice, but was insisting that there
was a greater gain than getting an inheritance, and a greater loss
than losing it. Possessions do not give life that is real life. That
comes from fellowship with God, who gives all that we have,
and to whom we are responsible for its use.

The rich fool looked upon his possessions as his own, not as
gifts from God. "*My* barns," "*my* grain," "*my* goods," "*my*
soul," he says (vss. 18-19). He made the mistake of thinking

that possessions make life. What would have been the meaning of "many years" of taking ease, eating, drinking, being merry? But little as possessions could give life, could they give even existence? Death separates from things. They cannot be taken with us beyond the portal, as evidence of a life worthily lived. God alone is Lord of life, and a person truly lives only when he is "rich toward God" in faith, obedience, and service (vss. 20-21).

Jesus pursues this thought further with his disciples. The faith which frees from covetousness frees from painful anxiety about the necessities of life (vs. 22). It does not, of course, free us from responsible toil and intelligent planning. An economy run on the basis of the life of birds and flowers would collapse. The point is that faith acknowledges even the fruits of toil as the gift of God, and therefore is free to labor without anxious care.

Three grounds are given for this: first, faith knows that life is in God's hands, and that gnawing anxiety is useless. As the birds and flowers are wholly dependent on providence, and can do nothing to create the means of their own sustenance, so man, with all his cleverness, cannot add one moment to the length of his life (vs. 25). How useless, then, is anxious concern! (vs. 26). Second, God's bounteous provision for things of a transient existence indicates his concern for man, who has an eternal destiny (vss. 27-28). Third, faith knows that God is more aware of our needs than we are, and that he is concerned that the needs of his children be met (vs. 30). The major aim of life, therefore, should be to continue to seek, in thought and life, the total Lordship of God over us and our society. With this concern made central, other needs will be fulfilled (vs. 31). This promise is for needs only, not desires; and for needs as God sees them, not as we see them. There is no final guarantee that men of faith will not suffer deprivation, even death.

Jesus' encouragement continued by assuring the disciples of the eternal certainty of the Kingdom. Even though their numbers may be small, their influence weak, and their enemies great, yet the Kingdom will be theirs because it is their "Father's good pleasure" (vs. 32). With confidence in this eternal Kingdom, the disciples should keep their interest in it quickened by sacrificial giving to others' needs. In such a life, one is laying up treasures which can never be taken away (vs. 33), and is ensuring that his heart stay drawn toward the eternal Kingdom (vs. 34).

Vigilant Hope (12:35-59)

Since the full coming of the Kingdom is in the future, two things are essential to those who are looking for it. Its delay demands continuing hope, and the absolute uncertainty of the time of its arrival requires constant vigilance. The disciples, then, are to be like servants who await the return of their master from a wedding (vs. 36). His coming may be delayed until very late in the night, for there is no telling when wedding guests may go home (vs. 38). But whenever he comes, early or late, those are blessed who are watchfully awaiting his arrival (vs. 37). The fact that the blessedness consists in sitting at table and being served by their master when he comes, indicates clearly that Jesus is speaking of himself (22:27). The final reward of watchful waiting is fellowship with him. Lest the delay in his coming should lull his followers into sloth, and divert their gaze to lesser things, they must remember that he will come as unexpectedly as a thief in the night (vss. 39-40; I Thess. 5:2; II Peter 3:10; Rev. 16:15). Unremitting vigilance, therefore, is necessary.

In response to a question from Peter (vs. 41), Jesus indicates that such watchfulness is especially necessary for those in a position of leadership. They are likened to servants left in charge of giving out the master's goods to other members of the household (vs. 42). Faithful discharge of their duties means larger service (vss. 43-44). But if the delay in the master's coming dulls their sense of watchfulness, and tends to make them act as masters instead of responsible servants of the master, their judgment will be heavy (vss. 45-46). The judgment of leaders will be correspondingly heavy, since more is required of them because of their privileged position (vss. 47-48; James 3:1).

The necessity of watchfulness is reinforced by the decisive nature of man's relation to Jesus. Jesus' references to "fire" and to "baptism" undoubtedly refer to his death and its consequences (vss. 49-50; Mark 10:38-40). John had described Jesus' work in terms of "fire" (Luke 3:9, 17). Jesus' earthly career did not fulfill this in the form which John expected. But his death and resurrection, as the decisive events of all history, became the fulcrum on which the destiny of individuals and nations turns. All must decide either for or against him. Hence, although he is the bringer of peace (1:79; 2:14; 7:50; 8:48; 19:38; John 14:27; 16:33; Eph. 2:14-18), it is a peace which for its fulfillment must await eternity. In history, his presence means division—a division which enters into the most sacred relationships (vss. 51-53; see also 2:34-35). Vigilant hope for his coming, therefore, may lead to the costly sacrifice of the most treasured of human ties.

The tragedy of Jesus' people was that they did not sense this decisiveness of his presence. They could predict the weather from wind and cloud, but were blind to the judgment which Jesus' presence was bringing (vss. 54-56). The root of their attitude was hypocrisy, religious externalism, formalism, unreality; they were content with superficial appearances, but unresponsive to the profound questions of the soul. Jesus tries to awaken them from their spiritual stupor by a warning. An accused person, making his way to the judge, can hardly escape the consequences when judgment sets in. The only possible escape is to settle with the accuser before official judgment falls (vss. 57-59). The details of the parable here cannot be pressed. It means only that God's judgment on his people is near. There is yet time to make a settlement by accepting Jesus as Messiah and Lord. If they refuse, judgment is inevitable. How terribly it came in A.D. 70!

Membership in the Kingdom (13:1—14:35)

A section of teaching is now introduced which shows clearly that membership in Jesus' Kingdom is based on quite different considerations from those which the Pharisees had laid down. Those whom they excluded—the lost sinners—were invited by Jesus into the Kingdom, while the Pharisees themselves were shut out unless they repented. What, therefore, is required for membership in Jesus' Kingdom?

Repentance (13:1—14:6)

Zealotism, the fanatical effort to bring the Messianic Age by armed revolt against Rome, stemmed from Galilee. It is likely, therefore, that either on a pilgrimage or during a feast, there was a messianic outbreak which Pilate ruthlessly put down. The Pharisees were at one with the Zealots in their desire to be rid of Rome, but rejected their use of force. With a theology which attributed individual suffering to individual sin, it was easy for the Pharisees to think that these Galileans were particularly wicked because of their use of force and therefore had been directly punished by God (vs. 2). The Zealots, on the other hand, would judge the workers on the tower in Siloam to have been particularly wicked. Pilate had built an aqueduct in Jerusalem, financed by funds from the sacred Temple tax. The Zealots would have considered work on this to be a fatal compromise with the Romans and a denial of loyalty to God, and could well have looked upon the accident as God's judgment (vs. 4).

Jesus insists that both Pharisee and Zealot were wrong, in that their conception of the Kingdom—whatever the method of bringing it—was self-centered. To both, the coming of the Kingdom meant merely the replacing of the Romans by the Jews as world conquerors. Unless they repented, changed their minds about the Kingdom, and laid aside the resistance to "the purpose of God" which they had manifested both toward John the Baptist and toward Jesus (7:30; 11:53-54), they would all perish (vss. 3, 5). In fact, were it not for the infinite patience of God, this would have happened already. The tree of Israel, which had not produced the fruits God expected, should before this have been cut down (vss. 6-7). But the time for repentance is now short. If fruit does not appear, the end will come (vss. 8-9). Repentance and acceptance of Jesus are immediate necessities.

The strong need for the repentance of the religious leaders is to be seen in the story of the Sabbath healing (vss. 10-17). A woman sorely afflicted for eighteen years, in a manner which seemed to be the direct work of an evil spirit (vss. 11, 16), was healed by Jesus. She immediately praised God. What could be more wholesome in the synagogue on the Sabbath, than that the works of Satan should be destroyed, and that men should lift their hearts to God in praise for this. The extent to which the religious leaders had missed the meaning of the Kingdom, and the testimony to it which their worship should have given, is shown in the fact that the ruler of the synagogue indignantly rebuked the people for coming to be healed on the Sabbath (vs. 14). There was hypocrisy in this. The ruler was really rebuking Jesus, but had not the courage to do it directly. Worse than that, however, was a hypocritical regard for the Law which objected to an incident that illustrated its deepest purpose—the glory of God Jewish tradition interpreted the Law more flexibly for animals than for man (vs. 15). Furthermore, the Sabbath, as God's day, would best be honored by doing God's work (vs. 16). A change of mind about the meaning of the Law was necessary before the Pharisees could enter the Kingdom.

Jesus knew that the likelihood of the repentance of official Judaism was not great. Two parables, therefore, are inserted here to show that in spite of this, the Kingdom would win its way. The growth of the mustard seed suggests the outer spread of the Kingdom to the ends of the earth (vss. 18-19), while the figure of the leaven depicts the inner power of the Kingdom to conquer all forms of evil (vss. 20-21). There is no indication that the process of growth would be automatic and continuous, written in the very nature of things. In Jesus' day, germination of seeds and the spread of leaven throughout the dough were commonly considered miraculous. The two parables, therefore, teach that the Kingdom will achieve its ends not by inevitable growth, but by the mysterious power hidden in Jesus.

Jesus' reply to the question concerning the number that would be saved continued to press the seriousness of the need for repentance on the part of those who felt themselves religiously secure (vss. 22-30). The number of the saved was a theoretical question often discussed by the rabbis. Jesus rejected all such speculative questions. He answered not the question, but the questioner. Obviously, the questioner assumed that he was numbered among the saved. Jesus sought to shake him loose by insisting that no one is saved by the accident of birth into the Jewish nation, nor by the achievement of keeping the Law. The door into salvation is narrow (vs. 24). Jesus himself is the Door (John 10:7-9). Repentance and faith in him are the only striving that counts. The door is too narrow to admit anyone who is loaded down with his own religious accomplishments.

Furthermore, there is a last judgment when the door will finally be shut (vs. 25). Then, those who are now indifferent to him who is the Door will seek to claim acquaintance with him (vs. 26). But their claim is superficial. External acquaintance, mere knowledge of his teaching, is not enough. One must know him in the deeper sense of repentance and faith, the turning away from the kind of self-justification which the questioner manifested, and the casting of the self on Jesus alone for salvation. All other acquaintance with him leads but to doom (vss. 27-28).

Israel's rejection of Jesus, however, does not thwart the plan of God. The true Israel is the Israel of "faith" (Rom. 4:16-25; Gal. 3:6-9), made up of both Jews and Gentiles who believe (vs. 29). The believing Gentiles, therefore, who were called last, will enter the Kingdom, while the unbelieving Jews, who were called first, will be shut out (vs. 30). The final criterion is not race, nor achievement, but repentance and faith.

The seriousness and immediacy of the need for repentance are reinforced by Jesus' reply to the warning about Herod's hostility (vs. 31). Both Herod's disposition and the report of it are natural at this time, for Jesus was probably in Perea, not far from the place where John had been arrested (3:19-20). Jesus replied that his career was determined not by Herod, no matter how sly he was, but by God. His Messianic work would be carried on until the precise time of its termination set by God (vs. 32).

The real danger of death for Jesus, however, lay with the religious leaders in Jerusalem (vs. 33). Jerusalem had almost a monopoly on killing prophets (II Kings 21:16; II Chron. 24:20-21; Jer. 26:20-23). Since Jesus must go on to make his final Messianic claim in the capital city, it was there that he would meet his fate. He had been there before, on visits not recorded by Luke (John 2-12), and had found only opposition and rejection (vs. 34). After their final rejection of him in the Crucifixion, God would reject them. Jerusalem would no longer be his city. It would be theirs alone! (vs. 35a). The final destruction of which the prophets spoke would come (Jer. 12:7; 22:5-9; Micah 3:12). But there is grace even in God's judgment. Although Jerusalem will be utterly rejected and destroyed, there will yet come a time in the future when at least some of God's ancient people, the Jews, will recognize in Jesus their Messiah, and bless him who has come in the name of the Lord (vs. 35b; Rom. 11:25-32). The gospel, which has come to the Gentiles through the defection of the Jews, will yet be accepted by Israel as "the power of God for salvation to every one who has faith" (Rom. 1:16).

A final example of the Pharisees' need for repentance is seen in another instance of Sabbath healing. Jesus challenged the Pharisees to acknowledge the act as a proper use of God's day (14:1-6). The need for repentance is seen in the self-centeredness of the Pharisees. They had more regard for a domestic animal which belonged to them, than for a stricken neighbor who belonged to God (vs. 5). Such egocentric use of God's Law is under judgment, and demands a radical change of mind. The silence of the Pharisees shows that they assented only reluctantly (vs. 6).

Humility (14:7-11)

The force of Jesus' teaching to the guests at dinner may be seen only when it is recognized as a parable (vs. 7). In itself, the principle that honors cannot be taken, but can only be received, is little more than a bit of social etiquette (vss. 8-10). Jesus meant more than that. The "marriage feast" is a parable of the Messianic Feast, the time of salvation, when those delivered by God would banquet with the Messiah (14:15). The principle that he who exalts himself will be humbled, but he who humbles himself will be exalted, indicates that in the Kingdom of God all values of this present order will be completely upset (vs. 11; 1:52; 15:18-32; 18:9-14; I Peter 5:5-6). Those whom God delights to honor confess that they have no right to status before God, and cast themselves wholly on him for mercy.

Disinterested Kindness (14:12-14)

Jesus' counsel to the host at dinner likewise involves more than etiquette. Jesus was not interested merely in who should be invited to a social occasion, but was striking at a major defect of Pharisaic piety. Pharisaism was a religion of merit, of salvation by works. By dint of human effort one earned what Paul called "a righteousness of my own, based on law" (Phil. 3:9). Good works were presented to God for an equivalent reward. Offering entertainment to others that they might invite one in return and thus repay the kindness, was an illustration of the Pharisees' relation to God. Jesus countered this by insisting that members of his Kingdom should act toward others as God had acted toward them (vss. 13-14). God gives to those who cannot requite him. His kindness goes out to those who can offer him nothing in return—but love. To act this way toward one's fellow man is to enter into the spirit and purpose of God, and is to be richly blessed at the final Judgment (vs. 14). Needless to say, if one should do kind deeds just *in order* to be repaid at the resurrection, the reward would not be his. It is those who act without thought of reward to whom the reward is given.

Response to God's Grace (14:15-24)

Jesus' mention of the resurrection (vs. 14) led a Pharisee to remark how blessed it would be when the Messianic Banquet took place (vs. 15). The tone of his remark suggested that there was no doubt that he and his companions would be numbered among the guests! Jesus sought to shatter his complacency and self-righteousness by the parable of the Banquet. It was customary in the East to have two invitations, one announcing the occasion ahead of time, the other reminding the guests at the appointed hour. The guests in the story had apparently accepted the first invitation, but when the second came, they insulted the host by begging off. It was a double insult, because it not only declined a previously accepted engagement, but the reasons given showed sheer contempt. Not one was valid (vss. 18-20).

The first invitation given was that of God's prophets, who had been announcing the coming of the Kingdom for generations. The final invitation, indicating that the Messianic Banquet was now ready, was the coming of Jesus. Jesus is warning the Pharisees that even though they had formally accepted God's prior invitation by considering themselves his people, their rejection of him now was a despicable refusal of God's offer of grace. They were preoccupied with lesser things, and were not really in a mood to respond to God's grace. Since no human host would react as did the one in the story, it is obvious that the host is God (vss. 21-23). His purpose is not to be thwarted, even though the Jewish people refuse his invitation. He will send his gracious summons to the Gentiles, until the last one has heard it. The solemn words of verse 24 are sobering. They suggest that it may be possible to reject God's grace irrevocably. To be invited is not enough. One must accept.

Total Commitment (14:25-35)

As Jesus continued journeying toward Jerusalem, "great multitudes" stayed close by him (vs. 25). They must have suspected that he was the Messiah, and wanted to be near him to share the joys of the Kingdom when it came. Like the dinner guest (vs. 15), they needed to learn that there was more involved than receiving benefits. The Kingdom makes demands. It is the Kingdom of the Suffering Servant. Membership in it, therefore, means sharing Christ's suffering and living as his servant. Jesus was on the way to the Cross. Those who followed him would have to be willing to bear a cross. This could mean separation from the most cherished loved ones—a separation as deep as that which hatred produces—if these interfered with loyalty to Jesus (vss. 26-27). The gospel deepens human love, and often natural affection and loyalty to Jesus are compatible (18:20; Matt. 15:4-9). But when there is a conflict, the claims of Jesus come first. Jesus' followers, therefore, should not be moved by mere emotion or motivated by easy hopes.

As building a tower is costly and waging war is dangerous, one must be willing deliberately to face both costliness and danger as Jesus' disciple (vss. 28-32). It means total renunciation of self, the readiness to offer up every precious thing if it is demanded in his service (vs. 33). This spirit of self-sacrifice for the sake of Jesus is the "salt" which preserves and sweetens society. Followers of Jesus who do not continue in a spirit of total commitment to him are worse than useless (vss. 34-35). Who can fail to hear the deep note of warning in Jesus' call to "hear"!

The God of the Kingdom (15:1-32)

The Pharisees and their scribes (interpreters of the Law) murmured against Jesus because he welcomed the "tax collectors and sinners" who did not keep the minute religious prescriptions which they had laid down (vss. 1-2). Jesus replied by three parables, all of which teach one central truth: *God loves sinners!* Our sin, rather than destroying God's interest in us, makes his love all the more intense. The Pharisees, therefore, were wrong about Jesus because they were wrong about God.

The Lost Sheep and the Lost Coin (15:3-10)

The "or" of verse 8 indicates that these two parables belong together, as two illustrations of the same point—a favorite teaching device of Jesus (13:18-21; 14:28-32). In both stories the emphasis is on the ones seeking the lost—the shepherd who has lost his sheep, the woman who has lost her coin. Three features of their search are depicted. First, its diligence. Search is made until the lost is found (vss. 4, 8). If one is lost it cannot be because God has not found him, but because he has refused to be taken back. Second, the tenderness of the searcher is depicted (vs. 5). The shepherd is God, who is depicted in Isaiah 40:11 as One who "will gather the lambs in his arms, he will carry them in his bosom." Third, the joy of finding is paramount (vss. 6, 9). Heaven's estimate of the worth of "tax collectors and sinners" is quite different from that of the Pharisees (vss. 7, 10).

It is not certain whether by "righteous persons" (vs. 7) Jesus means those who have already repented and are thus at home in the Father's house, or whether he is ironically referring to those who, by their scrupulous observance of the Pharisaic traditions, feel no need for repentance. The latter is likely, inasmuch as the whole chapter is directed toward the Pharisees' wrong estimate of the character of God. In either case, the truth remains that nothing so rejoices the heart of God as the repentance of a sinner. The agonizing concern over the loss of the sheep and the coin make their recovery a cause for greater rejoicing than the possession of those which were not lost.

The Lost Son (15:11-32)

The story of the Prodigal Son is really that of a father who lost two sons. Both boys, the one who strayed and the one who stayed, were lost to his love. It is possible that the one who stayed was the more lost. There is a new dimension here which could not enter into the other stories, and that is rebellion against love. The sheep was lost by heedless wandering and the inanimate coin had nothing to do with its own fate. But the sons are lost by their deliberate choice. The filial relation is refused. A breach of love is chosen. The dimension of sin and guilt enter here.

The sin of the younger son began in his choice to break the filial ties and to pursue life independently of his father. Although a father could voluntarily have divided his estate at an early time, yet it was normal custom for the heirs to receive their share at the death of the father (Heb. 9:16-17). The prodigal's sin, therefore, did not consist in wasting his part of the inheritance. This careless behavior was merely a symptom of the deep desire to be his own master, to live independently of his father's will, to do as he pleased, to shed the protective influences of home and love as unworthy of his own free manhood. In this was re-enacted the Fall of man. To succumb to the temptation to "be like God" (Gen. 3:5)—that is the story of humanity from the beginning to the present. The essence of sin is man's refusal to use God's gifts for God's glory, living as an obedient creature under the sovereign love of his Creator. But the will to be free enslaves. The prodigal came to want—friendless, forlorn, wretched, occupied with the lowliest task a Jew could assume (vss. 14-16).

Although the love of the father was seeking the son just as diligently as the shepherd and the woman sought, yet because of the moral nature of the relationship involved, the reconciliation had to await the son's change of heart. Heretofore he had been "beside himself." Now, "he came to himself" (vs. 17). And in this change is seen the meaning of true repentance. No longer grasping for his father's riches, he was content to turn from his disobedience and be an obedient servant of his father (vss. 18-19). Such repentance leads to forgiveness. Trudging wearily back home in the full knowledge that he had no right to be received by his father and no claim on his love, he finds his father looking for him, and more than ready to reinstate him into full sonship (vss. 22-24). His father not only meets his needs, but does him more honor than when he was at home before. The "best robe" was a sign of special honor, the "ring on his hand" was a sign of restored sonship, as were the shoes, for slaves wore no shoes. Forgiveness means not only the lifting of punishment and the setting aside of guilt; it means also full restoration to sonship (Gal. 4:5; Eph. 1:7; Col. 1:14).

This goes beyond all ideas of human justice. It is the grace of God. The elder brother, like the Pharisees, did not understand God's grace. He was basing his relation to his father on achievement and merit, seeking reward for his righteous deeds. He had served and obeyed. Why, then, should the prodigal be treated as well as or better than he? (vss. 29-30). He had no more of a relation of sonship to his father than did the prodigal. He had stayed under the father's roof but had not entered into the spirit of sonship. He served for reward rather than for love of his father. Thus, he could not understand the father's joy, which was the result not of the younger brother's achievement but of the fact that he had once more taken shelter in his love and had become a son. The father still loved the elder brother, and went out to entreat him to enter the family circle (vs. 28). But he could not refuse sonship to the prodigal because of his brother's objections. "It was fitting to make merry," for the dead was alive, the lost was found (vs. 32). In spite of the objection of the Pharisees, God must still welcome "tax collectors and sinners."

This is the gospel, but not the whole of it. These parables show only God's attitude of love toward sinners. But this attitude was depicted in Jesus' behavior as he was on the way to Jerusalem. Forgiveness finally meant the Cross! It could not be meted out with a gracious word alone. It must be given by a costly deed. Death and resurrection and the theology of atonement are involved in these simple and beautiful stories.

Warnings to Kingdom Members (16:1—18:30)

Some of the instruction of this section is given directly to the disciples, some to the Pharisees. In every instance, however, the truth is applicable to both groups. Jesus' upbraiding of the Pharisees, then, may well be taken as' a caution for those who claim kinship to him. Each ·item is a danger signal to believers.

Danger of Riches (16:1-31)

The outstanding symptom of the prodigal's independence of his father was the selfish use of possessions (15:13). For Kingdom members, therefore, the central mark of whose life should be obedience to God's will, the unselfish use of possessions for the good of others is demanded. This is set forth in an unusual but effective way in Jesus' story of the Unfaithful Steward (16:1-9). Threatened with dismissal, and unwilling either to work with his hands or to beg (vss. 2-3), the steward reduced the debts of his master's creditors, so that when he was dismissed they would show their gratitude by caring for him (vss. 4-7).

Jesus obviously did not approve the dishonesty of the steward (see vs. 10), but commended solely his prudence (vs. 8); that is, his wise use of present opportunities in a way which resulted in his future welfare. For the Christian, prudent use of possessions is to give them generously for the welfare of others (vs. 9). The expression "unrighteous mammon" does not mean ill-gotten gain. It is an expression corresponding to our "filthy lucre," and suggests that money belongs to the order of this present evil world which is perishing and has no permanent meaning (I John 2:17). "Eternal habitations" means "heaven." Jesus was not suggesting that anyone earns heaven by giving. Pharisaism held that heaven was a reward for good works. It was this which Jesus was combating. He was here indicating that one's use of possessions is a good test of his true relation to God. As a person of wealth entrusts part of his estate to his son to test him before giving him the whole inheritance, so God tests our fitness for the "true riches" of heaven in our use of material possessions (vss. 10-12). Our use of money is a good test of our acceptance of his Lordship. If we allow money to rule us, and make it a rival lord, it is evident that God's Lordship has not been wholly accepted (vs. 13). Since God is God, he can brook no rivals.

The Pharisees made sport of Jesus' teaching on riches (vs.

14). They looked upon wealth as the reward for righteousness, for keeping the Law, rather than as a danger. Jesus replied that it might be thus considered in the eyes of men, but not of God. Their religious praise of wealth was an effort to cover up hearts filled with greed (vs. 15; 20:47). Furthermore, the thought that men could be justified by keeping the Law had lost validity since the preaching of John. Repentance and belief in the good news of the Kingdom were the means of being justified before God. Now everyone, be he Pharisee or tax collector, scribe or harlot, could enter the Kingdom if he desired to press into it (vs. 16). This was not to say that the will of God expressed in the Law was set aside. Rather, it was fulfilled at a higher level (vs. 17; Matt. 5:17). Their efforts, therefore, to avoid the moral implications of God's Law by keeping the letter of it, as their divorce practices illustrated, were proof that riches in their case were no sign of God's approval (vs. 18).

To reinforce this, Jesus told the story of the rich man who failed to use his wealth under God's Lordship, and found it finally to be a great curse (vss. 19-31). The Pharisees accepted as normal the fact that plenty and poverty should dwell side by side, and were not concerned to change the situation. Plenty was a sign of God's favor, poverty a sign of his judgment (see Job 4:7-8; 8:6-7; Luke 13:2-5; John 9:1-3). The reason for such judgment was considered a hidden mystery known only to God, and man need not concern himself with it. Jesus' story was told to show that God did not reason this way. Possessions are given by him in trust, to be used as an expression of his concern for the needy. If one does not do this, it is clear that possessions, rather than God, are his lord. The interpretation should be limited to this. Attempts to picture the afterlife from it should be avoided.

It is to be noted, too, that the story does not condemn the rich man just because he was rich. Verse 25 must not be mechanically interpreted to mean that all the rich in this life suffer in the next and that all the poor in this life are blessed in the next. He is condemned purely because he failed to use his wealth in the service of God by concerning himself with the sufferings of his fellow men. A poor man would be likewise condemned if he behaved in the same way to a brother man still poorer.

The story is really a call to the Pharisees to repent of their external loyalty to the Law, and to turn their hearts toward finding the will of God expressed in it. They were scrupulously loyal to the current interpretation of the Law, but had not used it as an expression of God's Lordship over their lives. Their self-centered use of wealth was one of the clearest indications of this. The rich man's desire that his brothers "repent" (vss. 27-30) indicates that he had discovered that he was in hell not because he was rich, but because he had failed to repent of self-lordship and place himself under the Lordship of God. The major stress of the story, therefore, is found in Abraham's insistence that "Moses and the prophets" are sufficient to guide men to God, if they are willing to repent (vs. 31). Startling signs were neither necessary nor effective. Not even the resurrection of Jesus produced either repentance or faith on the part of the Pharisees. Their wealth and themselves were their lords, not God.

The warning is contemporary. Our attitude toward possessions is perhaps the clearest indication of whether or not we have repented of our self-centeredness and accepted God's total Lordship. And whoever conscientiously examines the hold that things have over him can only bow in penitence. It is a sobering thought, too, that our acceptance or rejection of God's Lordship in this life is decisive. There may be a "too late" (vss. 24-26).

Danger of Unbrotherly Behavior (17:1-6)

The realism of Jesus is to be seen in his certainty that, sin being what it is, brother would sin against brother in the Church. His word of warning against this, however, is one of the strongest on record. For a Christian to sin is not a private affair. Others seeing him may justify themselves in the same behavior by his example. Irresponsibly to lead into evil a weaker brother or a child, whose instinct to imitation is strong, has no excuse for the Christian (vs. 1; Rom. 14:13-23). The seriousness with which Jesus took this is to be seen in his strong warning against being the cause of the spiritual ruin of another (vs. 2).

One of the best ways to remove causes of stumbling from the Christian fellowship is to practice the grace of forgiveness (vs. 3). "Seven times in the day" means without limit. Jesus' realism is to be seen again in 'the fact that forgiveness is dependent on repentance (vs. 4). Unrepented sin is to be branded as such (see Jesus' example by contrasting 7:47-50 with 7:40-46). The connection between faith and one's relation to his brother, in Jesus' later words to Peter (22:32), suggests that the Apostles' request for additional faith here was to fulfill the high demand of limitless forgiveness (vs. 5). Jesus' reply was to the effect that the amount of faith is not so important as its genuineness. The figure of transplanting the tree into the sea is a picture suggesting that genuine faith can accomplish what experience, reason, and probability would deny, if it is exercised within God's will (vs. 6).

Danger of Self-Esteem (17:7-10)

In the ancient world, servants did not work for wages. They were the property of their owners. Their task was to do the will of their masters, with no regard for their own desires and no thought of reward (vss. 7-9). Jesus used this feature of the economic life of his time as an illustration of the disciple's relation to his Lord. The task of the Christian is to serve in obedience to his Master, and to do what is commanded with all the powers which he possesses. He can never say that he has done more than his duty, and think of himself as one who could be considered praiseworthy. It is his duty to give his entire service to the One to whom he belongs (vs. 10).

This does not mean that the Christian's work is not necessary, or that there will not be rewards (6:23). The Master of the Christian is exceedingly compassionate, and even serves his servants (12:37; 22:27), a thing unheard of in antiquity (vs. 8). But this is all of grace, and not because his servants deserve it. When we have done our best, we can never claim that we have done one thing more than we ought to have done. All we are and have belongs to the Master by right. To serve him is our duty. But duty in Christ's service is privilege. It would be folly to draw from this illustration of the defective social life of the Roman Empire a pattern for society today. It is one of the gospel's chief glories that it has rooted out all forms of slavery wherever its full power has been released.

Danger of Ingratitude (17:11-19)

The details of the story of the ten lepers accord fully with Jewish law (see on 5:12-16). The lepers stayed apart, outside the village (Lev. 13:45-46). They called out to announce their presence, although in this instance they exchanged the cry "Unclean, unclean," for a petition for help (vs. 13). They sought to assuage their misery by staying together in a group (II Kings 7:3-15). Jesus sent them to the priests for examination (vs. 14; Lev. 14). The fact that one of them was a Samaritan (vs. 16) shows how tragedy ofttimes brings together those who are normally separated by an impassable gulf.

The stress of the story is not on the healing, but on its outcome. Ten were healed. Only one returned to praise God (vss. 15-18). The others, who were Jews, may have felt that as members of God's Chosen People, the gift of healing was their due. In any case, they received physical healing, but because of their ingratitude they missed the redemption which fellowship with Jesus brings. A better translation of verse 19 would be: "Your faith has saved you" (see 7:50), referring to salvation rather than health. The nine received physical healing. That which sets this one off from them is that his gratitude to the healer brought him into the true People of God.

Two things are evident here. One is that faith is the only basis for membership in God's Kingdom. Here, a Samaritan who was excluded by the Jews was brought into the fellowship of Jesus because he believed, while nine Jews who felt themselves to be already members of the Kingdom were excluded. The fellowship of believers transcends all human differences, and unites men through faith in Jesus. Second, it is frighteningly possible to receive Jesus' gracious gifts in vain. Ingratitude does not deny us his mercies. It denies us him! Jesus administered no punishment to the nine lepers for their ingratitude. He just left them with his gifts—and themselves. To have him without his mercies, would be better than to have his mercies without him.

Danger of False Security (17:20—18:8)

The Old Testament spoke much of the coming Kingdom of God, but gave no indication of the time of its arrival. Mingled hope and curiosity led the rabbis to speculate on the nature of the signs which would announce its nearness. It was natural, therefore, that the Pharisees should ask Jesus for his opinion on when the Kingdom was coming (vs. 20). His reply was twofold. First, it corrected their external, political idea of the Kingdom (vs. 20). Its arrival would not consist in the establishment of an earthly state, which could be located, and which men could observe with the eyes. The signs of the Kingdom's presence were spiritual and could be interpreted only by faith. Second, the Kingdom was already present in him (vs. 21). He, as the King of the Kingdom, had come, had cast out demons, healed the sick, and announced the "good news" that the Kingdom was there

(4:18-21; 11:20). If they had interpreted these deeds and his teaching rightly by faith, they would have known that the Kingdom was already in their midst in him.

The same subject is continued, but to the disciples (vss. 22-37). It is now, however, not a question of the beginning of the Kingdom in the coming of Jesus, but rather of its completion when he comes again as Son of man. Throughout the New Testament these two aspects of the Kingdom are present. Jesus could say that "the kingdom of God has come" (11:20), and yet he taught us to pray, "Thy kingdom come" (11:2). The Kingdom is already here in Jesus, but not yet here in its fullness. The Church, therefore, must proclaim the Kingdom's presence and live in its power, yet at the same time witness that it is yet to come in its fullness.

For this reason, Christians will often long for the coming of the final victory (vs. 22). They must, however, live by faith in its coming, when there are no signs of it. Those who are unwilling to live by faith, and who tamper with signs and programs and dates, are to be resolutely avoided (vs. 23). When the Kingdom finally comes, it will come as suddenly and decisively as lightning, and all will know it (vs. 24). In the meantime, believers must live in constant expectancy and readiness. Jesus' rejection and death will lead his enemies to be careless, for they will think that they have done away with him forever (vs. 25). Hence, as in the days of Noah and Lot, they will live as though he were not to be reckoned with (vss. 26-30; Gen. 6:5—7:24; 19:1-28). The ordinary pursuits of life are legitimate, but are not to be engaged in as though they were permanent, nor allowed to crowd out the constant readiness to part with them at the coming of the Kingdom. A loose hold on the present order makes for readiness for the coming order (vs. 31). The fate of Lot's wife is an example of what happens to those who are too much tied to the goods of this world (vs. 32; Gen. 19:26).

One must be prepared to abandon the values of this world, in order to gain the life eternal (vs. 33). Detachment from earthly goods is necessary to a strong attachment to heavenly things. When the decisive moment comes, there will be a great separation. Some will be taken into the Kingdom, others left outside. Their outward estate is quite similar—sleeping at night, working in the day (vss. 34-35). The only difference is that some have known the transitory nature of this life and have lived in expectancy of the age to come, while others have felt secure in the present age. To the question of the disciples about where this should take place, Jesus replied with a proverb. The fact that it will take place is all that we can or need to know, and not the time or place. As surely as the vulture finds a carcass, so surely will judgment come (vs. 37). Therefore, be always ready!

The best way of reminding ourselves of the impermanence of the present order and keeping our expectancy of the coming Kingdom sharp, while at the same time developing patient steadfastness in waiting for it, is to pray. The Kingdom may be long delayed in coming. Bitter suffering may be the lot of those who wait for it. The temptation to despair will be great. The sigh, "O Lord, how long?" will often be on the lips of Christians. The one resource against succumbing to such temptation is prayer. Should prayer cease, Christians would lose heart (18:1).

On the other hand, if continuing urgency in request could produce results from an unjust judge (vss. 2-5), how much more effective will it be with him who is called "the righteous judge"? (II Tim. 4:8). God's people, as defenseless as the widow, will be vindicated in their trust in his promises of the coming Kingdom (vs. 7). The widow was unknown to the judge. God's people are God's children. Her cause was one of human rights, administered by social custom. Their cause is that of God's Kingdom. She came to the judge frequently. They are to pray "day and night," living in a continual attitude of prayer. Such prayer will receive its answer. Even though deliverance is not immediately forthcoming (vs. 7b), this is not to be interpreted as God's refusal to answer. He "will vindicate them speedily" (vs. 8a). The vindication may not seem speedy to men, but in terms of his program, in which "one day is as a thousand years, and a thousand years as one day" (II Peter 3:8), God will act quickly and decisively. His delay is a mercy to the enemies of his people. Believers are not to fret at the delay, but to be faithful (vs. 8b).

Danger of Self-Trust (18:9-30)

The parable of the Pharisee and the Publican is connected with the preceding teaching in two ways. First, after showing the necessity of constant prayer, Jesus had to indicate that not all prayer is genuine. Second, the thought of the coming Kingdom led him to correct some false ideas about it. The Pharisees felt that by properly keeping the Law, they were preparing the way for God's Kingdom. God's deliverance would be a reward for man's behavior. Righteousness was a human achievement, not a gift of God's grace. Jesus told this parable to warn against those "who trusted in themselves that they were righteous" (vs. 9).

The Pharisee could commend himself to God. He did have worthy religious achievements of which to boast. His avoidance of evil behavior was noteworthy. He did not extort, deal unjustly, commit adultery, nor compromise with the Romans for a living as did the tax collectors (vs. 11). Positively, too, he had much to his credit. Although fasting was not prescribed by the Law, he engaged in it twice a week as an act of self-mortification for the sins of the people, of which he felt himself not guilty (5:33). Some of the Pharisees not only tithed the products of the soil and their animals, as the Law prescribed (Deut. 14:22-23), but tithed even what they bought, lest they make use of something which had not been tithed (vs. 12). There is no accusation of insincerity here. Paul is a good example of a wholly sincere Pharisee, who could boast that he lived "as to righteousness under the law blameless" (Phil. 3:6). But this was what he called "a righteousness of my own, based on law" (Phil. 3:9). It sought to establish right relations to God by self-achievement, and to reduce God's dealing with man to mathematical precision.

The tax collector, on the other hand, could claim no merit. He did not even engage in the customary form of lifting up his eyes to heaven in prayer (vs. 13; John 11:41; 17:1). He could only use the sign of guilt and mourning—beating the breast (23:48)—while confessing that he had no status whatever before God, that he was nothing but a miserable sinner, and that his only hope of a right relation to God lay not in anything he could do, but in God's mercy (vs. 13). Here is no self-trust, only repentance and trust in God. We have Jesus' word for it that "this man went down to his house justified rather than the other" (vs. 14). For whoever commends himself to God will be abased before him, "but he who humbles himself will be exalted." Humility and self-abasement open the door to God's mercy!

The point is reinforced by Jesus' dealing with little children (vss. 15-17). They were mere infants in arms, symbols of total dependence and insignificance. Why should these, who were so insignificant, take the time of Jesus from those who were important? (vs. 15). In this objection, the disciples indicated that they still felt that some sort of worthiness was necessary in order to claim the attention of their Master. But it is to such as these that the Kingdom belongs, said Jesus (vs. 16). Only those who receive the Kingdom as children can enter it (vs. 17). Jesus was not here speaking of some primal innocence of children (parents know that they are not "little angels"). He was rather saying that only those can receive the Kingdom who accept it as a gift, because they have no sense of their own value, can offer to God no resources of their own, and are wholly dependent on him. These are the "poor," whose is the Kingdom of God (6:20).

An illustration from life follows, making very concrete the danger of self-trust (vss. 18-30). The rich young man, perhaps a ruler in the synagogue (see 14:1), trusted in himself and the possibility of his achievements, not in God. When he addressed Jesus as "Good Teacher," Jesus had to remind him that if he had any goodness, it was because of his total dependence on God, and not because of his own achievement (vs. 19; see John 5:19-20). The reminder indicates immediately that Jesus saw that the young man had himself rather than God at the center of his life. To focus his attention on the need for making God and his will central, Jesus reminded the young man, as he had done with others on similar occasions (10:25-28; 16:29-31), of the commandments which express God's will (vs. 20). The self-trust of the young man is seen in his reply (vs. 21). With utter sincerity, he claimed that he had kept the commandments! And he felt capable of doing even more to ensure his salvation, if Jesus would only tell him what it should be!

In order to show him that self rather than God was really the center of his life, Jesus bade him surrender all his earthly security, and follow him (vs. 22). This involved the twofold response of making God central and of following Jesus, who was on the way to Jerusalem to reveal God in an act of complete dedication and self-giving. The young man's refusal indicates that his wealth —not God—was supreme to him (vs. 23). Jesus' dealings with Zacchaeus (19:1-10) show that he was not teaching that wealth in itself is evil. It is only the love of it, which makes it an idol in the place of God, that is wrong.

The strong hold that the goods of this life have on us is to be seen in Jesus' sad recognition of how difficult it is for one who is wealthy to put God first. In fact, apart from the grace of God, it is impossible—literally as impossible as it is for a camel to go through the eye of a needle (vss. 24-25). Since all either have wealth, or seem to be seeking it, does not this automatically rule out nearly all from salvation? (vs. 26). The power of God's grace to release men from the binding slavery of things is exalted in Jesus' reply (vs. 27). Peter's question (vs. 28) shows that even the disciples had not yet fully realized the meaning of God's grace. They were still thinking in terms of reward for achievement. Jesus did not condemn them. They had perhaps come as far as was possible then. He promises them that no offering or service in his Kingdom is in vain. These lead to fellowship in the people of God and to eternal life (vss. 29-30).

The King Moves Toward His Kingdom (18:31—19:27)

To indicate to the disciples that the rewards just mentioned are not to be the motive of service, Jesus reminds them once more of his coming sacrifice at Jerusalem. Obedience to the will of God, which his self-offering will express, is the sole motive of service. This last announcement of his suffering goes beyond the earlier ones (9:22, 44; 17:25), in that Jerusalem is specifically named as the place of his suffering; stress is laid on his death as the direct fulfillment of prophecy (see 22:22, 37; 24:25-27, 44-47); and the Romans are mentioned as those at whose hands he will be executed (vss. 31-33). This was all beyond the understanding of the disciples at this moment. "They did not grasp what was said" (vs. 34). It would take Good Friday, Easter, and Pentecost to fill it with meaning.

The story of the blind man at Jericho (vss. 35-43) has special significance. It is the beginning of Jesus' open claim to be Messiah. Formerly, he had spoken only indirectly of his mission, and had refused to allow others publicly to call him Messiah (4:35, 41; 9:21, 36). Now, a great crowd of pilgrims going up to the Passover is around him, many of whom believed that "the kingdom of God was to appear immediately" (19:11). Whatever their judgment of him may have been, there is little doubt that they felt that he would have some relation to the coming of the Kingdom. The blind man, who apparently had heard of Jesus' mighty works before, called Jesus the "Son of David" (vss. 38-39). This was a Messianic title (20:41). This time Jesus does not refuse the public acclamation as Messiah. In fact, he seems deliberately to draw it out, by stopping to speak with the blind man, when he could well have avoided it (vs. 40). His question to the blind man has a similar character (vs. 41). Did the blind man merely want some alms, or did his faith in Jesus lead him to believe that Jesus could open his eyes, which was one of the signs of the Messianic Age? (4:18; 7:21; Isa. 29:18; 35:5).

In responding to the man's faith in his Messianic power by healing him, and doing it deliberately as the Son of David, Jesus began his public declaration of Messiahship, which was carried forward at the Triumphal Entry, and finally led him to death (22:67-71). In so doing, Jesus took full responsibility for the Messianic demonstration which took place at his entrance into Jerusalem (19:28-40), and allowed his people to pin their Messianic hopes on him. How different his conception of Messiahship was from theirs, however, the Cross would reveal.

This difference is strongly depicted in Jesus' dealings with Zacchaeus (19:1-10). Jericho was situated on a main route to Judea and Egypt, and was an important customs center. Zacchaeus was "a chief tax collector, and rich" (vs. 2). According to the Judaism of that time, his calling excluded him from membership in the people of God who would benefit from Messiah's coming (see on 5:27-32). He was, therefore, kept away from Jesus not only by the pressure of the crowd, but by religious ostracism (vs. 7). He may have heard of Jesus' gracious dealings with fellow tax collectors (5:27-32; 15:1-2) and, desirous of seeing a rabbi whose attitude was so different from that to which he was accustomed, would let nothing stand in his way (vs. 4).

Jesus' friendliness toward him and his willingness to be a guest in his home—a shocking thing for a religious person to do!—led Zacchaeus to a total change of heart. Fellowship with Jesus broke the hold riches had on him, and led him to make restitution of anything wrongfully taken (vs. 8). This was spontaneous gratitude to Jesus, as well as a reflection of a new sense of values which he found in Jesus' presence. He was not asked to give up all his wealth, as was the rich ruler (18:22), nor to leave his business and home, as was Levi (5:27-28). He merely became a new man, living in God's grace, in his old circumstances.

Jesus was moving toward Jerusalem as Messiah. But his Messiahship differed from the people's expectation, in that he received as "a son of Abraham" one whom they had excluded (vs. 9), and set forth his mission in religious rather than political terms. He had come not to establish an earthly throne from which to rule the nations. He had come "to seek and to save the lost" (vs. 10). It was this that would be achieved by what was shortly to transpire at Jerusalem. Tragically, it carried with it the self-exclusion of those who rejected him (13:27-30). In Zacchaeus and those who murmured against him is enacted in real life the parable of the Prodigal and the Elder Brother (15:11-32).

Jesus' last teaching before arriving in Jerusalem was directed mainly to his disciples, but had overtones of application to the Jewish nation which was soon to crown its rejection of him as Messiah by condemning him to death (vss. 11-27). Jesus' disciples had left home and employment, and had followed him through the months with increasing hope. Now that they were nearing Jerusalem, their hopes were fanned into flame. They thought that the Kingdom "was to appear immediately" (vs. 11), and that they would share in the glory of him who brought it (9:46, 49, 54; 18:28). Jesus had to show them that there would be a long period of waiting before the Kingdom came in all its glory. In the meantime, they were to serve responsibly in the midst of a hostile environment. Their final share in the Kingdom would depend on their faithfulness during the time of waiting.

The form of the parable is probably taken from a first-century event. Upon the death of Herod the Great, his son Archelaus made the long journey to Rome to have his rule over Judea confirmed by Augustus Caesar (vs. 12). The Jewish people sent a delegation at the same time, saying, "We do not want this man to reign over us" (vs. 14). The comparison is clear. Jesus, as he has intimated all along and as his disciples believe, will receive the Kingdom. But, as he has announced before and they did not understand (18:31-34), he must go on the long journey of death to receive this Kingdom. Later, he would return in "kingly power" (vs. 15; 23:42). In the meantime, his servants would have to live in the hostile environment of people who hate him (vs. 14). During this period, they were to take what they had received from him, and increase it by making disciples of all others who would hear them and believe (vs. 13). A reckoning would be made at his return (vs. 15). All bear the same responsibility, yet the results are not the same (vss. 16-24).

The only servants judged, however, are those who have merely kept intact what they received, and have made no effort to increase it (vss. 20-24). What they have will be given to those who have been faithful to their stewardship (vs. 24). The parenthetical remark of verse 25 was probably made by the listeners.

Jesus stated, in reply to their objection, a principle which he had laid down before (8:18)—unused gifts diminish, whereas those who use well what they have, find it continually growing. It is to be noted that the reward of the faithful is not mere restful inactivity and indulgent enjoyment; it is rather larger service (vss. 17-19). Verse 27 pictures the terrible fate of Jerusalem, which indicates the inexorable judgments of God in history, and stands as a warning for all who refuse God's mercy in Christ.

Jesus' teaching, both to the disciples and to the Jewish people, is now done. The arrival at Jerusalem is at hand. In what takes place there will be seen the meaning of all that he has done and has taught previously, and of all that he will continue to do and to teach until the end of the age.

MESSIAH MANIFESTS HIMSELF AT JERUSALEM: DEATH AND RESURRECTION OF THE SERVANT

Luke 19:28—24:53

This is the climactic section of the Gospel, to which everything has been pointing since Jesus' coming into the world. It is the record of Jesus' offering himself to his people in Jerusalem as their Messiah, their rejection of him which led to his death, and God's triumph over their rejection in the Resurrection. Jesus' rejection by his own people, however, was but a dramatic representation of his rejection by all men. Neither Jew nor Gentile was solely responsible for the death of Jesus. Both were party to the crime. Nor were only those who directly participated in the act responsible. They were simply a cross-section of humanity, representatives of us all. "All have sinned," and "the whole world may be held accountable to God" (Rom. 3:23 and 19). The story moves with little comment or interpretation on the part of Luke. The facts carry their own weight, both of judgment on human sin and of unspeakable mercy on God's part. Here the judgment of the world and its redemption meet in the most tragic, yet the most glorious, moment of God's saving action in behalf of man.

The Dramatic Arrival (19:28-48)

Jesus' arrival at Jerusalem was a dramatic moment. It was the point toward which he had been moving with determined intention for months (see 9:51). Fully aware that death would be the result, he chose to make an open proclamation of himself as God's Messiah in God's city. The events associated with his dramatic arrival sprang the trap which led him to the Cross.

The Triumphal Entry (19:28-40)

The Triumphal Entry was definitely a Messianic act. It was Jesus' offering of himself to his people as their Messiah in a way which they must either accept or reject. The deliberateness of this act is to be seen in the precise arrangements Jesus made for it (vss. 30-31). The fact that the colt had more than one owner (vs. 33) may suggest their poverty. Their willingness to let the animal go because "the Lord" needed it may indicate some previous knowledge of Jesus on their part (vs. 34).

Every feature of the story indicates Jesus' intention to declare himself as Israel's King. The place is significant (vs. 37). Zechariah had spoken of a time when "the LORD will become king over all the earth." "On that day his feet shall stand on the Mount of Olives" (Zech. 14:9 and 4). Evidence that this passage had stirred hopes of God's deliverance of his people is to be seen in the fact that in the days of Nero an Egyptian Jew rallied a multitude of followers to storm the walls of Jerusalem from the Mount of Olives (see Acts 21:38). Jesus, therefore, appeared on this Mount to proclaim himself Israel's true Deliverer.

That the colt was to be one "on which no one has ever yet sat" (vs. 30) further shows the special significance of this occasion to Jesus. Animals which had never been used were commandeered for especially holy purposes (see Num. 19:2; Deut. 21:3; I Sam. 6:7). Furthermore, the whole event was a conscious enactment of an ancient prophecy: "Lo, your king comes to you . . . humble and riding on an ass" (Zech. 9:9). That Jesus was dramatizing this ancient prophecy is to be seen in his words to his disciples not long before: "Behold, we are going up to Jerusalem, and everything that is written of the Son of man by the prophets will be accomplished" (18:31). Jesus' every act during his last days was a conscious fulfillment of a divine plan to which the Old Testament bore witness.

That the disciples and the accompanying multitude caught the Messianic significance of all this is to be seen in two facts. First, they cast their garments on the road before him (vs. 36). This was an act of homage rendered to royalty (see II Kings 9:13).

Second, as the Holy City came into sight the whole multitude burst out spontaneously in praise to God in the words of Psalm 118: "Blessed be the King who comes in the name of the Lord!" (vs. 38; Ps. 118:26). Psalm 118, embodying their hopes of God's coming deliverance, was sung by pilgrims on the way to the Jerusalem feasts. Now the Deliverer was here!

That Jesus planned his entrance into Jerusalem as a Messianic act is to be seen further in his reply to the Pharisees who asked him to rebuke the disciples (vss. 39-40). They cautioned him against stirring up the Romans through such a frenzied outburst, which they regarded also as a religious scandal. Jesus' reply indicated that he fully accepted the Messianic ovation given him (vs. 40). Using a proverbial expression (see Hab. 2:11), he insisted that the homage was legitimate. He was saying, in effect: Messiah is here, and somebody must herald his coming. It could not be that there would take place the momentous event toward which the entire Old Testament, even the entire history of mankind, had been moving, without some recognition of its happening. Should men not herald it, the very stones would cry out. The secret of Jesus' Messiahship, which heretofore he had kept to himself and had not permitted either demons or disciples to proclaim (4:35, 41; 9:21, 36), must be revealed before his death. The issue is clear. Israel must either accept or reject her Messiah.

The Lament Over Jerusalem (19:41-44)

Although Jesus accepted the Messianic ovation given him, he alone knew how mistaken it was and how short-lived it would be. As at the Great Confession he had accepted the disciples' verdict of Messiahship, yet immediately reinterpreted it in terms of the suffering Son of man (9:20-22), so here he accepts the adulation of the multitudes but at the same time knows that it means something far different from what they think. He was Israel's King, but his Kingdom was "not of this world" (John 18:36). The crowds were looking for political deliverance from Rome; he had come to bring spiritual deliverance from sin. They wanted One to conquer Caesar; he had come to conquer Satan. He knew that this meant humiliation, suffering, death. He knew, too, that their mistaken political hopes would be blasted in a divine judgment on them for refusing to accept the deliverance from sin which God had brought in him. Hence, in the midst of adulation and the contagious rejoicing of the crowds, Jesus wept (vs. 41).

Jerusalem was to Jesus a much-loved city. It was the city where God had chosen to establish his presence among men. It was the center of a Temple, a Law, and a People which held the spiritual hopes of humanity and which were dear to Jesus. But it was a city blind to God's will and purpose, a rebellious city which did not know "the things that make for peace" (vs. 42)—the proposal of reconciliation which God had made to them in Jesus. God had "visited" them with offers of grace, but they did not know it (vs. 44; see also Gen. 50:24 for the meaning of "visit"). Consequently, nothing lay ahead but judgment. The Romans would attack the city and utterly destroy it. Jesus must speak this word of judgment, but he weeps as he does it. He had no tears for his own suffering which was soon to come, but his heart broke over his people whom he had come to save. To be the means of the destruction of the very people he had come to redeem, was to Jesus a part of the Cross.

The Cleansing of the Temple (19:45-48)

If there was any doubt left about Jesus' intention in the Triumphal Entry, it was decisively removed by his action in cleansing the Temple. As it was expected that the Messiah would come from the Mount of Olives (see the discussion of 19:37), it was also thought that he would openly declare himself in the Temple (Mal. 3:1). Here Jesus, in conscious fulfillment of prophecy, declared himself with dramatic suddenness. Furthermore, his action in driving from the Temple those who were defiling it as a business center, was wholly in accord with Malachi's description. He was to "purify the sons of Levi and refine them like gold and silver, till they present right offerings to the LORD" (Mal. 3:3). Jesus' attack on the High Priesthood here could hardly have been a more exact fulfillment of this prophetic word.

For the sake of enriching the Temple treasury, the High Priest Annas had established a lively business in the sale of animals for sacrifice, and in the exchange of foreign money into Jewish money, in which the Temple tax had to be paid. This business was carried on in the Court of the Gentiles, the outer court of the Temple. Operating as a virtual monopoly, and with an assured market, the chief priests profited greatly from the enterprise.

Jesus' assumption of complete authority over this priestly misuse of the Temple was a claim to Messiahship. That this claim prompted his action, rather than a sudden outburst of uncontrollable temper, is to be seen in Mark's word that Jesus "looked round at everything" in the Temple, then went out to spend the night before taking action (11:11). His deed came, therefore, after long deliberation. Jesus based his action on reasonable grounds drawn from Scripture (vs. 46). The Second Isaiah had described the Temple as a "house of prayer" (Isa. 56:7). For the priests, whose business it was to assist men in bringing their offerings to God, to place economic considerations above worship, was a misuse of God's house which Messiah could not tolerate. The second passage of Scripture on which Jesus based his action suggests that there may even have been a measure of fraud in the whole affair. To examine the context in which Jeremiah says that God's house had "become a den of robbers" (Jer. 7:11), makes it difficult to avoid the conclusion that this is what Jesus had in mind.

God's Messiah had come "like a refiner's fire" (Mal. 3:2), to claim God's rights in his house. In Messiah's presence, the Temple became once more a "house of prayer" where men could pour out their hearts to God. But more than that, it became also a place where God could speak to men. Consequently, Jesus "was teaching daily in the temple" (19:47), setting forth both by what he said and by what he was the whole truth of God.

By his direct claim to authority in God's house, Jesus forced his death. He was not of the priestly clan. He had no credentials from the Jerusalem authorities which gave him rights in God's house. The issue was squarely joined. Either he had rights there because he was the Messiah, or he must be destroyed. Consequently, "the chief priests and the scribes and the principal men of the people sought to destroy him" (vs. 47). It was of these three groups that the Sanhedrin, the highest court of authority among the Jews, consisted. They could not take immediate action because of Jesus' popularity with the multitudes. Many of the common people thought him to be Messiah, and in an open contest would have stood with him against the authorities. Furthermore, the cleansing of the Temple was an act which had the support of almost all save the high officials themselves. The ordinary priests opposed the business traffic in the Temple (see 1:5-6), while the people were solidly set against it. Consequently, a temporary shield of protection was thrown around Jesus. The protection, however, would soon be torn away, and Jesus would go to the Cross. Jerusalem did not know the time of her "visitation" (vs. 44).

The Temple Ministry (20:1—21:38)

The protection of the crowds gave Jesus opportunity to teach in the Temple for a few days. During this period the authorities pressed him with questions designed to discredit him with the multitudes, or to entice him into answers which might lead to his condemnation on religious grounds according to the Jewish Law, or on political grounds according to Roman Law (see vs. 20). After he had silenced their questions (vs. 40), he confronted them with further claims (vss. 41-44), offered some additional instruction (vss. 45-47; 21:1-4), and then gave a discourse on the destruction of Jerusalem and the End of the Age (21:5-38).

By What Authority? (20:1-18)

Responding to Jesus' act in cleansing the Temple, the authorities began their counterattack. It showed the marks of careful planning, both because it was made by "the chief priests and the scribes with the elders" (20:1), who composed the Sanhedrin, and because the nature of the question was cleverly designed, as would be expected from legal experts (vs. 2). At least two motives lay behind the question. First, if Jesus were to be taken, it was necessary to discredit him before the people. If he could be exposed as having acted without proper credentials, this end might be achieved. Second, if Jesus could be induced to make a verbal claim to Messiahship, they might condemn him for blasphemy.

Four elements were included in Jesus' counterquestion. First, he was trying to show them that the problem of spiritual authority is not one that can be settled by mere objective considerations, nor by authoritarian answers. John had come announcing the nearness of the Kingdom of God, but the religious leaders had not committed themselves to his message (vs. 5; see 7:30). If they were unwilling to make a commitment, no claim to authority on Jesus' part would be convincing. If authority is *from God*, I must surrender to it before I can rightly judge it. Jesus' questioners got the point. "If we say, 'From heaven,' he will say, 'Why did you not *believe* him?' " (vs. 5).

Second, John's baptism was a call to repentance. It involved not theological, but *moral*, decision. Was God at work in John? Since the mission of John and that of Jesus were bound together (see 7:33-35), a moral decision about John was necessary before the issue of Jesus could be settled.

Third, Jesus was making an offer of himself to them. He asked
his counterquestion to see whether they would open their hearts
to him. Mutual trust is necessary before the mystery of Jesus'
Person can be made known.

Fourth, Jesus made an indirect but clear answer to their question. John had appeared as a prophet. If he were not from God,
then he was an imposter. If he were genuine, the renewal of
prophecy in him was a sign of the beginning of the Messianic
Age. His pointing to Jesus as the Coming One was evidence, to
those who were willing to receive it, that Jesus was the Messiah.
Hence, still avoiding a verbal claim to Messiahship, as was his
custom, Jesus answered their question by indirection. Their effort
to discredit him before the people ended in failure.

Jesus now told a parable to reinforce the truth that the rejection of both John and himself by the religious leaders would
bring drastic judgment (vss. 9-18). The figure of a vineyard was
a familiar representation of Israel (see Isa. 5:1-7; Jer. 12:10;
Hosea 10:1; Ps. 80:8-13). It suggested both God's choice, for a
vineyard does not plant itself, and God's patient nurture of his
people, inasmuch as a vineyard needs constant care. The fruit of
obedience to his will is a legitimate demand on God's part.

The story is a rehearsal of the history of God's dealing with
his people. The tenants are the leaders of Israel, who had the
spiritual life of the people in their charge. The servants who are
sent in succession are the prophets. The fact that judgment did
not come at the initial rejection is a clear reflection of the patience and love of God for his people. This is underlined by the
fact that God then did what no human owner would have done
—sent his "beloved son" in the hope that the tenants might respond to him (vs. 13). The expression clearly refers to Jesus
(see 3:22; 9:35). The love of God surpasses all human calculation and knowledge. It is difficult to know in what sense the
tenants thought the "inheritance" was to pass to them if the son
were killed (vs. 14). This may reflect the very essence of sin,
which according to Genesis 3:5 is man's desire to be "like God,"
in the sense of being independent of him by refusing to live under his sovereign will. One of the greatest mysteries of sin is the
fact that the desire for independence from God can often take
the form of religious activity.

The destruction of the tenants means that the vineyard will be
given to others (vs. 16). The rebellion of Israel does not thwart

the purpose of God. It will go forward through the Gentiles, who are also the objects of God's grace (see Isa. 42:6; 49:6; Rom. 9-11). This drew from the people the spontaneous expression, "God forbid!" (vs. 16). To them it was unthinkable that the purpose of God could be transferred to any people other than the Jews. Jesus, therefore, drew upon Psalm 118:22, a Messianic Psalm, implying that he was the stone which the builders of Israel would reject, but that God would make him the cornerstone of a New Israel, the Church (see Acts 4:11; I Cor. 3:16; Eph. 2:19-22; I Peter 2:4-8). Even if Israel rejected their Messiah, the purpose of God would be fulfilled, and Jesus' authority would remain. The Son who came to offer himself on the altar of God's love also gave some terrible warnings (vs. 18). The smoldering heap of ruins which was Jerusalem in A.D. 70 testified to the fact that the warning here was more than mere words.

Tribute to Caesar? (20:19-26)

Thwarted in their first attempt to trap Jesus, and angered by Jesus' words of judgment on them, the scribes and chief priests were held back from seizing him immediately only by their fear of stirring up an insurrection among the people (vs. 19). They would try another tack. They would seek to involve him in trouble with the Roman governor. To that end, they sent spies whose purpose it was to catch him in some word which would lead to his condemnation by Pilate (vs. 20).

The attack opened with insincere flattery over Jesus' proclamation of the truth without fear or favor (vs. 21). Then the spies sought to place Jesus in a dilemma, so that he would be condemned whichever way he replied (vs. 22). If Jesus approved paying the tax, he would incur the disfavor of the people by appearing to be unconcerned about the burden Rome had placed on them, as well as indifferent to God's Lordship as supreme over that of Caesar. On the other hand, if Jesus denied the lawfulness of paying the Roman tax, he could be reported to Pilate, who dealt summarily with such people.

Jesus was not deceived by their "craftiness" (vs. 23). He asked for a coin, pointed out Caesar's likeness inscribed on it, and replied: "Then render to Caesar the things that are Caesar's, and to God the things that are God's" (vss. 24-25). Although the Zealots based their tax resistance on religious grounds, there is little doubt that economic motives entered into it also. Jesus,

therefore, was suggesting that one should not confuse the claims
of Mammon with those of God. Furthermore, the resistance to
Roman taxation was based on a political conception of the Kingdom of God. The Zealots—and even the Pharisees, who were not
so extreme in their views—equated the coming of the Kingdom
with freedom from Rome. Jesus was here intimating that the
Kingdom did not depend on political deliverance from Rome.
They could offer to God their whole loyalty within the framework of the Roman government. Deliverance was there through
a Messiah who was not to battle against Rome, but was to surrender himself to the suffering of the Cross, and thus call to himself a new People who would see that the Kingdom had come in
his deliverance from sin and death.

The ruse had failed. Jesus had not been caught on the horns
of the dilemma they had posed. He had said nothing by which
he could be discredited either with the people or with Pilate. His
questioners could but marvel and remain silent (vs. 26).

Is There a Resurrection? (20:27-40)

The Sadducees now tried to trap Jesus. The first attempt had
been to discredit him with the people, the second, to involve him
in treason against Rome. The third took the form of ridicule. It
involved more than that, however. The Sadducees, who were the
priestly aristocracy, held only the Law—that is, the Five Books
of Moses—to be authoritative. The Pharisees, on the other hand,
added the Prophets and other writings of the Old Testament to
the Law, as well as the oral tradition which had grown up around
them. One of the leading theological points on which the two
groups differed was that of the resurrection of the dead. Moses
had said nothing about it; therefore, to the Sadducees, it could
not be true (vs. 27; see also Acts 4:1-2; 23:6-10). If Jesus held
to it, along with the Pharisees, they could accuse him of conflict
with Moses, the authoritative teacher of the Law, and of conflict
with divine revelation. Furthermore, the Pharisaic belief in the
resurrection could be reduced to absurdity by an example.

To assure posterity to the dead, the brother of a man who died
without children was to take his wife and raise up children in his
name (Deut. 25:5-6). An imaginary case was conjured up in
which this happened seven times with the same woman. "In the
resurrection, therefore, whose wife will the woman be?" (vs.
33). The first part of Jesus' answer was a corrective of the Phar-

isees' view of the resurrection, which permitted the Sadducees to pose such absurdities. The Pharisees had pictured heaven as a mere continuation of this world, a heightening of all the normal functions of life as we know it here. Jesus insists, however, that the resurrection world is not merely a perfecting of this world. It is *another* world, different from this—God's world, which is beyond our understanding (vss. 34-36). It is a world as different from ours as God differs from man (see I Cor. 15:35-50; Phil. 3:21). Marriage is designed for this world to fulfill the social needs of man (Gen. 2:18-25) and for the procreation of the race (Gen. 1:28). In the world of the resurrection where death is no more, the second is superfluous and the first will be fulfilled, in a fellowship with God like that of the angels. Hence, the question they have posed is absurd not because there is no resurrection, but because they did not understand its nature.

The second part of Jesus' answer was directed to the Sadducees. It is a strong affirmation of the resurrection of the dead, based on the very Scriptures which they had used to deny it—the writings of Moses, and not from some obscure, insignificant passage, but from the very fountainhead of God's revelation to Moses at the burning bush (vss. 37-38; Exod. 3:1-6). Since God is the Creator, who has life in himself and can know no death, then all those who have been related to him by faith share in his life. Faith in the resurrection, therefore, depends on faith in God. Is the God in whom we believe the living God? Then those who are in him live! No one dared to question Jesus further, for each time he gained an advantage which put his opponents to shame (vss. 39-40).

David's Son or David's Lord? (20:41-44)

Having silenced his opponents, Jesus now challenged them to think through the question of his Messiahship at a deeper level. The political Messianic hopes of the scribes pictured the "Son of David" as one who would re-establish the throne of David and rule over an earthly kingdom. Jesus accepted the title "Son of David" for himself (18:37, 39), and the Early Church held him to be such (see 1:69; 3:31; Rom. 1:3; II Tim. 2:8). But both Jesus and the Early Church lifted this title above political ideas, and set it in the context of Jesus' Lordship over all authorities and powers, whether in this world or the world to come (Eph. 1:20-22; Col. 1:12-20). The total Lordship of Jesus, over this world and the unseen world, over the living and the dead, over things present and things to come, was established through his resurrection from the dead (Rom. 1:4; I Cor. 15:20-28; I Peter 3:21-22). But to be raised from the dead, it was necessary for him to die. As Messiah who had come to die, therefore, he could not reign as a political deliverer, but must be humiliated, rejected, despised, condemned (see 9:22, 44-45; 17:25; 18:31-33; Isa. 53; Phil. 2:5-11). It was this humiliation and lowliness, this failure to use political power to free them from the Romans, which led the Jews to reject his Messianic claims.

To show that such humiliation really did not speak against his Messiahship, Jesus referred them to Psalm 110:1, a verse which all interpreted as Messianic. There, Messiah is referred to as David's Lord rather than David's Son. This means two things. First, there is more to true Messiahship than to be a political heir to the throne of David. Second, the expression "David's Son" as referring to the Messiah really involved an aspect of humiliation rather than exaltation. The exaltation of the Messiah is not that of David's Son, but is the exaltation which makes him David's Lord and Lord of all the kings of the earth. His exaltation is to be seated at the right hand of God, not to rule on an earthly throne. As David's Son, then, he must be humiliated, in order that he may be raised to God's right hand to reign until all enemies are put under his feet. This was a challenge to the scribes to rethink the nature of Messiahship, and to see in Jesus' humiliation not a sign that he was not David's Son, but a sign that he was exactly that, and was also David's Lord.

Beware of the Scribes (20:45-47)

Jesus continued his reproach against the scribes, warning his disciples in the presence of all the people against their false piety. Three aspects of it are here singled out. The first was their personal ambition (vs. 46). In the Orient, positions of honor are marked by outward signs. One's dress, the greetings given him on the street, the location of his seat in the synagogue or at a feast, all indicate the relative position of honor in which one is held. To covet public honors was wholly out of accord with the religion of the lowly Son of man who "came not to be served but to serve" (Mark 10:45; see also Luke 22:27). Second, Jesus reproved their greed (vs. 47a; see also 16:13-15). The Law had ordained special concern for widows and orphans (Exod. 22:

22-24). It was doubly blameworthy, then, when those who claimed to be the guardians of the Law tried to evade it by profiting at the expense of those whose interests they were to guard. Third, there was religious hypocrisy (vs. 47b). Prayers evaluated by their length rather than their depth, and made to impress men rather than God, were strongly condemned by Jesus (see 18:9-14; Matt. 6:5-15).

Because of the scribes' position as teachers of the Law, their condemnation for disregard of the Law will be all the greater (vs. 47c; see also James 3:1).

The Widow's Offering (21:1-4)

The connection between this incident and the condemnation of the scribes which immediately precedes it is clear. In contrast to a piety which paraded in public for self-gain, the poor widow gave all she had in love for God. The widow had too little for display, and her offering could in no sense have been prompted by selfishness. It was too small for notice—about a quarter of a cent—save for the penetrating eye of Jesus. His praise for her act was as great as his condemnation of the scribes (vss. 3-4).

The radical difference between Jesus' evaluation of her gift and the customary evaluation is to be seen in the fact that he measured it not by its amount, but by *what she had left!* The generosity of those who give freely is good. But when large amounts are left for the giver, the value in God's sight is less than that of a small gift from one who has little left for himself.

Foregleams of the Future (21:5-38)

As one stands on a high mountain, viewing an ever-receding range of peaks, seeing only the broad features and unable to measure the distances between them, so apocalyptic vision sees the broad features of the coming pattern without precise detail, and with events sometimes blending without attention to the time which separates them. Hence, in this passage the fall of Jerusalem and the End of the Age so blend that the features of each cannot be precisely determined.

The discourse arose out of a remark of the disciples about the "noble stones and offerings" of the Temple (vs. 5). It was a magnificent set of buildings, with both beauty and size which would dwarf most modern religious structures. Its forty-foot columns carved out of single stones, its "offerings" such as Herod's

golden vine with clusters taller than a man, and its gold-covered
dome, made it a source of pride to every Jew in the world. It
was also the center of their hopes. It was the place where God
had chosen to dwell, the God on whom they relied for deliverance from their enemies. And in spite of Roman occupation they
were still free to carry on their worship without Roman inter-
ference. The Temple, therefore, was the one remaining symbol
of God's Lordship, and their one hope of deliverance from Rome.

It was a startling thing for Jesus to respond to their remark
by abruptly announcing the total destruction of all this (vs. 6).
In so doing, he was following in the footsteps of Jeremiah, who
had predicted the destruction of the former Temple (26:6). According to Matthew (24:1) and Mark (13:1), the saying was
made only in the presence of the disciples. If it became known,
it would have been just grounds for demanding his death. (It
seems to have played some part in his trial; see Mark 14:58;
15:29. Did Judas make it known?) The response of the people
to Jeremiah was: "You shall die!" (Jer. 26:8). To announce the
ruin of the Temple was to say that Israel would cease being the
people of God. And since the Jews could not conceive of the existence of God without his people to adore him, this was to them
blasphemy against God.

The question of the disciples about when this should happen
and what its sign should be, suggests that they did not catch the
full force of his meaning (vs. 7). There was a current expectation of a time of "woes" or "sufferings" prior to the coming of
the Messianic Age, which would be the birthpangs of the new
order (see Matt. 24:8; Mark 13:8). The disciples, therefore,
may have thought that Jesus referred to this, which would be not
the annihilation of the Temple, but its removal for an even more
glorious one to befit Messiah's Kingdom. Jesus' answer gives no
specific hints about time, and cautions against any confidence in
so-called "signs" of coming events. There will be many who will
arise, saying that the "signs of the times" point to such and such
events, and some will even offer themselves as God's Messiah
(vs. 8). Furthermore, there will be international unrest and wars
to reckon with. These are in God's plan, but are not to bring
terror to God's people (vs. 9). They are not to be interpreted as
signs that the end is near. Jesus seems to be counseling both to
discernment and to patience. The necessity of this is to be seen
in the fact that during the next few decades there were false mes-

siahs who arose to lead many astray by proclaiming that the decisive moment of history was at hand (see Acts 21:38).

Another description of coming wars is given, to which is added further signs of the terrible disruption of life which will cause distress among the Jews—earthquakes, famine, pestilence, and terrors in the heavens (vss. 10-11). These latter are frequently used in apocalyptic writing to describe the intensity of events, and are not to be taken literally (see Acts 2:16-21).

But before the fall of Jerusalem, the Church will be called upon to suffer for the name of Christ, both from Jews and Gentiles (vs. 12). The Book of the Acts bears abundant testimony to the truth of this (see, for example, 4:1-22; 5:17-40; 7:1-60; 14:19; 16:19-24). Yet the persecution was to be an opportunity for the Christians to "bear testimony" to their faith (vs. 13), and would be a time when they would discover the presence of their Lord in a most intimate and helpful way (vss. 14-15; see also Acts 4:13; 6:10).

Their power to witness, however, was no guarantee against further persecution. In fact, the most precious ties of life would in some cases have to be broken, and they would frequently know the hatred of all men (vss. 16-17). This was a part of the cost of following their suffering Lord which he had formerly announced to them (see 9:23-27), and must be endured to the end (vs. 19). The encouragement to endurance lay in the fact that it was for his sake, and in his promise of protecting grace at all times (vs. 18). It did not mean, of course, protection from physical harm, for he had already told them that some of them would be "put to death" (vs. 16). It must mean, rather, what Paul was speaking of in Romans when he insisted that no peril in life or in death, in this world or the next, can "separate us from the love of God in Christ Jesus our Lord" (Rom. 8:39).

The discourse proceeds at this point to advise Jesus' followers about what to do when the siege of Jerusalem comes. When the armies of Rome surround the city, there will be no possible defense. Therefore, those who are in the province of Judea should escape to the mountains, those who are in the environs of Jerusalem should not enter the city, and those who are in the city should flee (vss. 20-21). For Jerusalem's doom is sure. It is the judgment of God (vs. 22).

When Jerusalem was attacked in A.D. 66-70, the Christians followed this counsel of their Lord, leaving Jerusalem for Pella, east of the Jordan. The Jews, on the other hand, fanatically expected that God would intervene to save them. They cried to God to the last—but no help came. The wall was breached, the Temple went up in flames, and the city was decimated. How clearly Jesus saw all this coming, and with what pathos he described the future suffering of the inhabitants of the city! (vss. 23-24). The interval between the fall of Jerusalem and the End of the Age is called "the times of the Gentiles," during which the gospel is announced to the Gentiles and the vineyard is given to others than the Jews (see 20:16; 13:29-30).

The discourse now turns to the End of the Age and the coming of the Son of man. (For the meaning of this term see the discussion of 5:24.) The view broadens to take in the whole of creation. The vivid description of turbulence is perhaps not to be taken literally (vss. 25-28). It is the sort of language frequently used in the Old Testament to describe violent change and to suggest the coming of a totally new order—the Day of the Lord (see Isa. 13:9-16; Joel 2:10, 30-31). Jesus will finally come "with power and great glory" to be acknowledged by the whole universe as Lord (vs. 27). The coming "in a cloud" is an apocalyptic form, suggesting his arrival from the unseen realm (see I Thess. 4:16-17). What form this will take is impossible for us to understand with our finite minds. The mood for believers who await the final End is to be one of hope. It is difficult to know to what the expression "these things" in verse 28 refers, but it would seem to relate to the calamities incident to the destruction of Jerusalem. But in all the turbulence of history prior to the End, Christians are to see the hand of God at work, and to know that their redemption is continually "drawing near."

As the appearance of the leaves on the trees augurs the sure coming of summer before it arrives, so God's judgments in history are signs that his Kingdom is near (vss. 29-31). History is moving toward the End which God has set for it. The final assurance of this cannot rest on observation of events or any reasoned calculation. It rests rather on the sure word of Jesus, whose words will abide when "heaven and earth . . . pass away" (vs. 33). If verse 32 can be referred to the destruction of Jerusalem, it presents no problem, for that took place within the lifetime of many to whom Jesus was speaking. If it does not relate to that, it presents us with an almost insoluble problem, for Jesus did not make guesses about the date of the End (see Mark 13:32).

Hope should be accompanied by watchfulness, in awaiting the End. For it will come with suddenness, like the springing of a trap, which gives no evidence of its presence until it clamps its iron jaws on its victim (vs. 34). And it will come upon all (vs. 35). Constant preparedness is the only safe mood under such circumstances. One must therefore avoid dulling his spiritual sensibilities by indulgence or overconcern for material things (see also 12:13-31, 35-48; 17:26-37). There must be believing prayer, to keep one aware of the realities of the unseen world and open the channels of life to the gift of God's strength, without which no one may "stand before the Son of man" (vs. 36; see also 18:1-8; Rom. 8:26-39; Eph. 6:18; Phil. 4:6-7).

Verses 37 and 38 give a brief summary of Jesus' last days in Jerusalem. He taught in the Temple by day. He went to the Mount of Olives by night, possibly to avoid secret arrest before the time of his suffering came, and certainly to have opportunity for uninterrupted prayer and communion with his Father (see 22:39-40). The people remained loyal to him, rising early in the morning to hear him teach, and still casting around him a bulwark of protection from the religious leaders (see 22:2).

Feb 9

Last Hours with the Disciples (22:1-38)

All four of the Gospels indicate that Jesus spent the last hours before his arrest with his disciples. The desire to be alone with the inner circle at the last arose both from the natural reluctance to part with these who had continued with him in his "trials" (vs. 28), and from the desire to do what he could to prepare them for the cruel blow which was soon to follow.

The Treachery of Judas (22:1-6)

The story of Jesus' last hours with the disciples is introduced by the treachery of Judas. Luke uses no words of condemnation. It was judgment enough merely to say that he "was of the number of the twelve" (vs. 3). Although technically the Passover, which lasted one day, is distinguished from the Feast of Unleavened Bread, which came on the seven days immediately following, the two were popularly named as one (see Matt. 26:17).

In seeking to put Jesus to death, the religious leaders were faced with a difficult situation. The Passover was at hand. The Galileans who came to the feasts were easily aroused to fanatical

action which the Romans, goaded by the extreme Zealots, took
very seriously and had on previous occasions put down with the
sword (see 13:1). Ever since the Triumphal Entry, the attitude
of the Galilean pilgrims had been threatening. If Jesus were not
put away quickly, an uprising might occur among his followers
and the consequences would be bloody. If things broke out on a
large scale, the Romans might even decide to take decisive action
and destroy their holy place and their nation (John 11:48).

The leaders held a secret meeting in the High Priest's palace
to determine on a course of action (vs. 2; see also Matt. 26:3-4).
At this moment help came from an unexpected source. Judas
appeared and offered to betray Jesus (vs. 4). The "captains"
were members of the priestly aristocracy in charge of the Temple
guard and responsible for order in the Temple area (see Acts
4:1; 5:24, 26). Judas' coming naturally caused great rejoicing,
and they showed their appreciation by offering him money for
his services. In what did Judas' betrayal consist? In the promise
to lead them to where Jesus spent the night, so that they could
take him "in the absence of the multitude" (vs. 6; see also John
18:2). He may also have reported what Jesus said to his disciples
about the destruction of the Temple (21:6), which might be used
as evidence of blasphemy (see Mark 14:58; 15:29).

The records are strangely silent about interpreting the cause
of Judas' deed. Luke seems content to see in it the mystery of
sin. "Satan entered into Judas," he tells us (vs. 3; see also John
13:2, 27). If we could explain Judas' action, we could explain
sin. And, as Luther remarked, if we could explain sin, we would
do away with it. The mystery of sin is known only to God. But
Judas is a warning that no position of Christian privilege is im-
mune from temptation and fall. He illustrates Bunyan's comment
that there is "a way to hell from the very gate of heaven."

Did Judas have to betray Jesus? The record does not say so.
On the other hand, it gives every evidence that he did not. All
the scheming of the officials and the conniving of Judas were unnecessary. Jesus had come to Jerusalem to die (9:22, 43-45, 51;
17:25; 18:31-34). There was, therefore, no need to plot against
him. In the last analysis, it was Jesus, not Judas, who determined
the time of his death.

The Last Supper (22:7-23)

Thousands of pilgrims descended on Jerusalem for the Passover Feast. The meal was celebrated in groups of not less than ten. Jerusalem homes were opened to pilgrims for this purpose. Peter and John, two of the most trusted disciples, were sent to make the necessary preparations (vss. 8-12). Even they would not know the place until they got there. Judas would not know it until the Supper took place, so that he could do his evil deed only after he had been there and left (see John 13:30).

The intense "desire" (vs. 15) of Jesus to eat this Passover with his disciples had two grounds. First, the final struggle with evil which lay between him and victory, forbidding as it was (see vs. 44), lured him. As the knowledge of a coming crisis may make a soldier impatient to meet it, so he could not rest until the dark hour which lay before him had been met. Second, inasmuch as what he was going to accomplish was for the new People of God, of which the disciples were the nucleus, Jesus wanted to celebrate the Passover with them in a way which would give it a new fullness of meaning.

Both the eating of the Passover meal (vs. 16) and the drinking of the Passover wine (vss. 17-18) were to be "fulfilled in the kingdom of God." That which the Passover foreshadowed was to become a reality through him. Paul called Christ "our paschal lamb" (I Cor. 5:7). The Passover represented God's deliverance of his people from Egypt (Exod. 12:1—13:10). A greater deliverance was now about to take place in Jesus—deliverance from sin. The celebration of the earlier deliverance on this occasion was invested with a new meaning on the verge of its fulfillment. So the sadness of farewell was also the joy of the coming Kingdom. The Lord's Supper continues to be an anticipation of the coming Messianic Banquet, when Jesus shall return to complete the work he has accomplished in his death and resurrection. "For as often as you eat this bread and drink the cup, you proclaim the Lord's death *until he comes*" (I Cor. 11:26).

At this point in the Passover meal, Jesus instituted something new—the sacrament of the Lord's Supper (vss. 19-20; it seems preferable to leave vss. 19b and 20 in the text). As the bread was broken, so was his body to be broken for the sake of his disciples ("given for you," vs. 19, margin; the "you" including the whole Church, of which the disciples were representative). As the Old

Covenant between God and men had been ratified by blood (Exod. 24:1-8), here was a New Covenant ratified by Jesus' own blood, a Covenant which could never be broken (vs. 20, margin). As the Old Covenant had brought into being the ancient People of God (Exod. 19:3-6; Deut. 7:6-8; 14:2), here was a New Covenant to bring into being a new People of God (II Cor. 3:6-18; Titus 2:14; I Peter 2:9-10).

In these words instituting the Lord's Supper there is also a reference to the Suffering Servant, who is to be the instrument of the New Covenant. For the Servant was the one through whom the Covenant was to be renewed and given to "the nations" (Isa. 42:6; 49:6, 8).

Membership in the new People of God through the forgiveness of sins is Christ's gift. "He broke it and *gave* it to them" (vs. 19). He does this still in the Lord's Supper. To partake of the bread and wine is a "remembrance" of him (vs. 19, margin). But true "remembrance" involves participation with him in his death and resurrection, through the action of the Holy Spirit, if it is accompanied by faith (see I Cor. 10:16). Christ actually *gives himself* to his people in the Sacrament.

This giving, however, is conditioned not upon any worthiness but purely upon a willingness to receive. That is why Judas' betrayal is brought in at this point (vss. 21-23). If Luke has placed it right, then Judas partook of the Last Supper. In this act, Jesus was trying to get him to renew his loyalty, to abandon his treacherous designs, that the Lord might give himself to him as to the others. But the gift cannot be forced. It must be gladly received in faith and a desire to be obedient to Jesus' will. The Sacrament without faith brings judgment (I Cor. 11:29). But neither Jesus' words nor his acts led Judas to repentance. All Jesus could do was to pronounce a doleful "woe" (vs. 22). It is a frightening fact that sin can poison the inner life without outward signs of its presence. None of the others suspected Judas.

The Last Teaching (22:24-38)

The disciples' questioning among themselves about who was the betrayer (vs. 23) is contrasted with a dispute about who should be "regarded as the greatest" (vs. 24). This indicates the terrible twist of the human heart which, rather than humbly facing its own lack, is inclined to vaunt itself over others.

Jesus settled their dispute by showing that in his Kingdom

there was a total reversal of the values of this world. In Gentile (political) kingdoms greatness consisted in ruling and in the honor of bearing the title of "benefactor" of the human race, through some noted deed for which a king's subjects honored him (vs. 25). In Jesus' Kingdom, however, true greatness is service without thought of honor or reward (vs. 26). The strongest reinforcement of this principle was Jesus' own example. Although in the kingdoms of this world, the great sit at table and are served, he, the truly Great One, was the One who served them (vs. 27).

Although the disciples were not to share in earthly glory, there was a yet greater glory reserved for them. They were to be privileged to sit at table with the Messiah in his Kingdom (vss. 29-30). The Messianic Age was frequently pictured in the form of a Messianic Banquet (13:29; 14:15-24; Rev. 19:7-9). Those, therefore, who had shared in the Last Supper would, through the death which that Supper signified, finally enjoy the full reality of the Kingdom of God. This is no offer of a cheap reward of position and privilege like those sought after in this world, only delayed to the next. The reward is *fellowship with Jesus!*

What is meant by the Apostles sitting "on thrones judging the twelve tribes of Israel" is not certain (vs. 30). It can hardly be taken literally, however, but is rather a word picture, as is eating and drinking at Jesus' table in the Kingdom. In any case, since whatever is meant is some special function in the Kingdom of him who rules by serving, it can only speak of some special service appointed to the Apostles, rather than some honor. The condition of blessedness is not learning, cleverness, accomplishment. It is to stand by Jesus in his "trials"—the costly way of rejection and suffering (vs. 28; see also Rom. 8:18-25; II Cor. 4:16-18; II Tim. 2:11-12).

Although the disciples thus far had continued with Jesus in his trials (vs. 28), the big test of their fidelity was yet to come. Jesus addresses Simon in speaking of this coming test, but the pronoun "you" is plural, indicating that all the disciples were included (vs. 31). The prayer of Jesus, too, was for all (see John 17:6-19). The use of "Simon" instead of "Peter" was perhaps a dramatic suggestion that he was shortly to act in a way more in accord with his old nature than with the new one promised him by Jesus (see John 1:42)—more like sand than rock. The words of Jesus suggest the deep dimension of the struggle in the human soul. More is involved than mere human forces. It is a battle between Satan and Jesus. Satan claimed the disciples, that he might subject them to the buffeting process of threshing grain. His hope was, of course, to crush them in the process. His request to test them was granted (compare Job 1:6-12; 2:1-6), but his end would not be achieved. The reason was that Jesus had entered the battle on the disciples' side. "I have prayed for you" (vs. 32). The only possible source of moral victory lies in Jesus' intercession for us—his baring his own breast to the blows of Satan, and saving us by his strength (Rom. 8:26-39).

Jesus did not pray that they would be spared from testing, but that during temptation and fall they would not fail utterly. The outcome of Peter's coming denial would be to make him the more able to strengthen his brethren (vs. 32).

Peter failed to understand the dimensions of the testing through which he and the others were to go. The surest way to failure is to underestimate the odds against us! The only response the warning drew from Peter was a self-confident assertion that he would stand by Jesus, even to the death (vs. 33). Had the battle been one of mere physical bravery, he would have made good on his claim (see 22:49-50; John 18:10). But the issue was deeper. It meant watching Jesus go to shameful defeat and death. Was Peter prepared to be loyal to him through that? Before the cock announced the morning light, Peter would three times deny that he ever knew Jesus (vs. 34).

Jesus' last word to the disciples before going to Gethsemane was a word of warning. The earlier days when they had had a welcome reception from those to whom they had gone would soon give way to struggle and suffering. He had sent them out earlier without provision for their own needs (9:1-5; 10:1-9), and those to whom they went had gladly received them and entertained them. They lacked "nothing" (vs. 35). But from now on, the hatred which is soon to break over Jesus will also engulf them. The Scripture which foretold the reckoning of the Suffering Servant with transgressors was about to have its fulfillment (vs. 37; see Isa. 53:12; Luke 23:32). That would be the signal for a battle against Jesus' followers. They, therefore, should be prepared for battle. They should take a purse for money, a bag for provisions, and a sword for battle (vs. 36).

These instructions are most certainly not to be taken literally, as the disciples at that time seemed to take them. They showed him two swords which they had previously concealed, to which

he answered, "It is enough" (vs. 38). If Jesus' reply were taken
literally, it would run counter to his teaching against the use of
force (6:27-29), it would be open to the absurdity that two
swords were enough for twelve men to use, and it would be in-
consistent with Jesus' behavior in the Garden of Gethsemane a
short time later (vss. 49-53). The words are symbolic. The disciples are to be prepared for a real battle for the sake of Jesus,
but a battle with no other sword than that of the gospel—"the
sword of the Spirit, which is the word of God" (Eph. 6:17).

Gethsemane (22:39-46)

Luke's account of the struggle in the Garden is brief, omitting
much that the other Gospels tell. It concentrates on the intensity
of Jesus' struggle. The fact that Jesus planned his own arrest is
seen in his going to the Garden on the slopes of the Mount of
Olives, "as was his custom" (vs. 39). He had been spending each
night there recently (21:37). He knew that Judas had gone to
inform the authorities where they might find him. Instead of
going elsewhere to avoid arrest, he went exactly where he had
been going, to the place Judas well knew (see John 18:2), to
await his seizure. He is master, not Judas and not the authorities.

As they enter the Garden, Jesus counsels the disciples to pray
in order not to succumb to the temptation which is soon to come
(vs. 40). They had shown him two swords (vs. 38). He tells
them that their only defense against temptation is prayer. Will
we who claim to be his disciples ever learn this? Jesus reinforced
his words by his own example. The one weapon of defense
which was his as this most tragic of hours came upon him was
prayer. We enter here upon a "deep, mysterious, and incom-
municable" moment in the life of Jesus. We are moving in the
unfathomable depths of the mystery of our redemption. A weight
of emotion began to come over Jesus which could not be shared
by the most intimate of companions. Hence, he withdrew from
the disciples to battle it out alone (vs. 41).

A "cup" is a common figure for experiences either of blessing
(Pss. 16:5; 23:5) or of cursing (Pss. 11:6; 75:8) which are
appointed for an individual or a whole people (Jer. 49:12). Here
Jesus faces the curse of death, and, shrinking from it, asks his
Father to remove it if possible, yet yields in perfect obedience to
his will if that cannot be (vs. 42). At this point the mystery

reaches its depth. It is quite natural that a vigorous thirty-year-old man should want to live. The will to live is the strongest drive of human nature. But there is much more involved than that. Death is the instrument of Satan, the order of the kingdom where he reigns. Jesus had come "to destroy the works of the devil" (I John 3:8). He had sent to John as evidence of his Messiahship the fact that "the dead are raised" (7:22). He had manifested his authority over Satan by invading his kingdom of death and raising the victims (7:11-15; 8:49-55; John 11). Now he himself was faced with submitting to Satan's power. He had triumphed over Satan at the Temptation, but now the "opportune time" for Satan to return had come (4:13), and the incongruity of it struck him with unbelievable force.

Satan made one last onslaught to try to turn him from the path of obedience to his Father. The Suffering Servant entered a deeper darkness than he could have imagined before it came. He must know in all its horror what the prophet meant when he described the Servant as one "who *walks in darkness and has no light,* yet trusts in the name of the LORD and relies upon his God" (Isa. 50:10). The darkness came over his soul. He must submit to the Evil One. He must pay "the wages of sin"—death (Rom. 6:23)— not for his own sins but to bear "the sin of many" (Isa. 53:12). He must make "himself an offering for sin" in order that he might "make many to be accounted righteous" (Isa. 53:10-11). He "who knew no sin," whose perfect holiness was the very antithesis of evil, had "for our sake" to be "made . . . sin . . . so that in him we might become the righteousness of God" (II Cor. 5:21).

It is a mark of Jesus' true humanity that he did not face this without a struggle. Yet the struggle was rooted in surrender to the Father's will—"nevertheless not my will, but thine, be done" (vs. 42). This oneness with the Father's will found its response in God, who sent an angel from heaven to strengthen him (vs. 43). The angel, however, did not come to lift the struggle, but to enable him to go through it at an even deeper depth. The struggle continues "in an agony" and in even more earnest prayer, until there were physical marks of the struggle in sweat "like great drops of blood" (vs. 44). But the disciples were sleeping! Luke accounts for this as a device to escape sorrow (vs. 45). A better means would have been to pray, for therein lies the only strength against temptation (vs. 46). There was, however, no time to pray now. The hour of Jesus' arrest had come.

The Passion (22:47—23:56)

At this point the Servant fulfills the mission of suffering for which he had come into the world. Luke is content to tell the story simply, with little interpretation, and to let the facts speak for themselves. A great deal of political intrigue, however, lies behind the facts and accounts for them. We shall try to point these out at appropriate places as we move through the story.

The Betrayal and Arrest (22:47-54a)

Judas led the "crowd" who came to arrest Jesus to the Garden of Gethsemane. He had arranged to identify Jesus with a kiss (vs. 47). Whether this was to hide his purpose from the other disciples, or whether hatred inspired Judas to turn the sign of affection into treason, the story does not say. In any case, Jesus knew his design, and tried to strike a blow on his conscience. He called him by name, he upbraided him for using a kiss for such false purposes, and reminded him that what he was doing was done against the "Son of man"—the Messiah (vs. 48).

When the other disciples sensed that Jesus was to be seized, they asked permission to defend him (vs. 49). Peter, however, never a man to wait for permission or to deliberate long before acting, drew the sword. Like a flash, it cut the air (vs. 50; John 18:10 identifies Peter). Fortunately, the nimble slave of the High Priest dodged in time to lose only an ear instead of his head. There was both bravery and loyalty in Peter's act. He had sworn to go to death with Jesus (22:33), and here he showed his willingness to make good on his vow. To take on an armed mob singlehanded is no sign of cowardice. But Peter's act was not one of faith. He could not leave things in the hands of his Lord, but acted in line with his own will and judgment. Jesus immediately rebuked him, and in order to save Peter from arrest, healed the slave's ear (vs. 51). There seems to have been no attempt to arrest the disciples. This is evidence that the charge that Jesus was leading a revolt against Rome was false.

Jesus then turned to address the leaders of the mob. The captains of the Temple (Jewish officers charged with arrests for religious reasons), elders (the leading representatives of the people, and members of the Sanhedrin), and the chief priests were all there (vs. 52). They seem also to have brought their slaves with them, and according to John there was also a group of

Roman soldiers present with their captain (John 18:3, 12). For this group to come to arrest Jesus, the soldiers armed with swords and the others with clubs, suggests either that the Jewish leaders were putting on a mock show of danger for the sake of the Romans, or were really afraid that Jesus' friends among the people might have gotten wind of their plans and would be present to stage an uprising. How ludicrous it all was! Such a mob to take one lone man, who was planning to give himself up in accordance with a higher will than theirs!

The word "robber" (vs. 52) likely meant a Zealot who was prepared to take fanatical political action against Rome (see 23:18-19, 25; John 18:40). Jesus rebuked the Jewish leaders for thus representing him to the Romans. He reminded them that he had taught openly in the Temple day after day, and they could find no charge which justified condemnation (vs. 53). For them, therefore, to represent him to the Romans as politically dangerous was utterly false. Furthermore, their inability to take him before, although they were more than eager to do so (19: 47-48; 20:19-20; 22:2), shows that Jesus was not really in their power. They could do nothing to him except by his own decision to accept it. But God had permitted all this, had temporarily turned things over to them, and was subjecting his Son to all that they could do. They were tools in the hands of the "power of darkness" which was now making its final effort to destroy Jesus (vs. 53). But the power of darkness would be broken. "God's passion is his action." It would be light on Easter.

Peter's Denial (22:54b-62)

What went on in the soul of Peter that night would be hard to tell. A strong, physically brave man, ready to attack a mob in defense of his best friend, but rebuffed by the very One he sought to save, Peter must have put up his sword in disappointment and confusion of spirit. When he saw his Master led off toward the city, he could not resist following and mingling with the crowd to see what would happen. John tells us that the maid who blurted out to the group that Peter was one of Jesus' friends was the doorkeeper who had let Peter in at the request of another disciple (John 18:16). This is confirmed by her use of the word "also" (vs. 56). Peter denied that he even knew Jesus (vs. 57). Twice later he made denials, two of them at least with an interval of an hour between them. The futility of his denials, however, lay in the fact that his Galilean dialect betrayed him (vs. 59). Peter had failed to heed Jesus' warning (vss. 31-34), or to take his advice about praying for strength to overcome temptation (vss. 40, 46). Self-reliance leads always to moral failure.

Two things brought Peter up short. First, the crowing of the cock reminded him of Jesus' warning (vss. 60, 34). Second, as the cock crowed, Jesus—who stood shackled within the court or was being led to the quarters of Caiaphas—"turned and looked at Peter" (vs. 61). It was Jesus' steadfast love in spite of his denial which broke Peter's heart. Jesus' look brought back his words of warning (vs. 61). It must also have brought back other words. "Simon, Simon, behold, Satan demanded to have you . . . and when you have turned . . . " (vss. 31-32). Despair led to hope. The tears of this strong man (vs. 62) "washed his soul back to God." It is not without significance that Peter was the first of the Apostles to whom the risen Lord appeared (24:34).

The Jewish Trial (22:63-71)

Luke omits the fact that two informal trials of Jesus were held during the night, shortly after his arrest: the first a personal inquisition by Annas, the most influential member of the priestly group (John 18:13, 19-24), and the second before the hurriedly assembled Sanhedrin (Mark 14:53-65). Since a sentence of death could not be passed at night, they must await the coming of day to take formal action on what they had already determined informally. In the meantime, the guards who had Jesus in charge whiled away the tedious hours by making sport of him. With ridicule, physical torture, and religious mockery, they subjected the most sensitive person who ever lived to the crassest and most vulgar brutality (vss. 63-65).

When day came, the Council, composed of seventy-one elders (leading citizens), chief priests (Sadducees), and scribes (Pharisees), assembled for official action (vs. 66). The Romans had granted to them power of judging their own people on religious questions. A sentence of death, however, could not be carried out without Roman approval. Their problem, then, was to produce some evidence whereby Jesus could be certified as politically dangerous to the Romans. They therefore confronted Jesus straightforwardly: "If you are the Christ, tell us" (vs. 67).

Jesus' reply could be neither Yes nor No. A Yes would have meant that he was the sort of political Messiah of which they were thinking. Nothing could have been further from his mind. A No, on the other hand, would have been false, for he was Messiah. If he asked them questions to draw out their own Messianic views in order to correct them, they would not discuss with him, as a former occasion had shown (20:7; see also 20:41-44). On the other hand, if he told them of the true nature of his Messiahship, they were not capable of understanding it, because they would not believe (vss. 67-68).

In the knowledge, therefore, that discussion was futile, and to avoid any misunderstanding about the political nature of his Messiahship, Jesus changed the word "Messiah" or Christ, to "Son of man," his favorite title for himself (see on 5:24). Drawing upon Daniel 7:13 and Psalm 110:1, he made the bold assertion that from now on—as the result of his coming death—he would be seated at God's right hand, an expression meaning to share God's power and authority (vs. 69). In this the Sanhedrin sensed an even higher claim than that of Messiah. "Are you the Son of God, then?" they asked (vs. 70). Again, Jesus made reply in a fashion that neither openly affirmed nor denied. To affirm would have been to admit the charge placed against him in the Fourth Gospel, that he made "himself equal with God" (John 5:18). Jesus could not well here explain, as he did there, that this equality was one growing out of a mutual love between him and the Father, and his absolute obedience to his Father's will (John 5:19-20). On the other hand, to have denied Sonship to God would have been false. Hence he says, "You say that I am" (vs. 70). You affirm it, not I; but I do not deny it. The Sanhedrin caught the admission of Sonship to God, which to them was blasphemy. No need to proceed further. His own lips had condemned him (vs. 71). The only thing left to do now was to procure his death at the hands of Pilate.

The Roman Trial (23:1-25)

At the conclusion of the Jewish trial, the whole Sanhedrin moved over to Pilate's judgment hall. It was still very early in the morning (John 18:28). Three charges against Jesus were laid before Pilate. Since death could not be procured on grounds of mere religious blasphemy, the charges were all political: first, encouraging the people to sedition; second, forbidding the payment of the Roman tax; third, claiming to be a Messianic King (vs. 2). The first of these charges was wholly false. The

second was the exact opposite of the public teaching of Jesus
(20:21-25). The third was true, but not in the sense in which
they represented it to Pilate. For Jesus had renounced every
claim to political Messiahship, the only thing which could be of
concern to the Romans.

Unable, however, to appear indifferent to a charge of political
treason, lest he be misrepresented to Tiberius Caesar, Pilate put
to Jesus the question: "Are you the King of the Jews?" (vs. 3).
The answer of Jesus may be interpreted as a straightforward affirmation—"What you said is true!"—or it may have been another case of an answer with a double meaning—"*You* said it,
not I, for I am a different sort of King from the kind your words
imply" (see John 18:36-37, where Jesus told Pilate that he was
King of the kingdom of truth). In any case, Pilate is convinced
that Jesus is not politically dangerous, and seeks to dismiss the
case (vs. 4). The Jewish leaders, however, are not to be put off so
easily. They accuse Jesus more urgently, claiming that he had
fostered sedition all the way from Galilee, where most seditious
movements had their beginning, clear to Jerusalem (vs. 5; the
term "all Judea" here probably includes the whole of Palestine
rather than merely the southern province).

The shrewd ears of Pilate heard the word "Galilee" gladly.
If Jesus was a Galilean, then he came from the jurisdiction of
Herod Antipas, who had but lately come on a visit to Jerusalem.
A twofold motive led Pilate to send Jesus to Herod for judgment.
It would take a very unpleasant case off his hands, and by this
gesture of respect for Herod, it would heal a personal breach
between them which had arisen possibly through Pilate's bru-
tally putting to death some of Herod's subjects (13:1).

Herod was overjoyed at seeing Jesus, a prospect which he had
anticipated for a long time (9:9). He had formerly held conver-
sations with John the Baptist (Mark 6:20), but unfortunately for
him, John did no miracles (John 10:41). He hoped, therefore, to
see a display of the miracle-working power of Jesus about which
he had heard (vs. 8). It is not surprising that Jesus made no reply
to one thus depraved (vs. 9).

The Jewish leaders, afraid lest Herod might acquit Jesus or
send him back to Pilate with a recommendation of release, ve-
hemently pressed their charges (vs. 10). Jesus' silence was re-
warded by Herod with contemptuous mockery. In a gesture of
mutual courtesy, Herod renounced jurisdiction over his subject,

and returned him to Pilate, clothed in a gorgeous robe. This was a part of his mockery, and indicated to Pilate that Herod took no more seriously than he the danger of Jesus as a king (vs. 11). Through this exchange of mutual courtesies, Pilate and Herod healed their quarrel, each no doubt hoping thereby to advance his own political interests (vs. 12).

Pilate still had Jesus on his hands. None of the charges brought against him was true, and he had no reason to condemn him (vs. 14). In order, however, to satisfy the Jews that he was not indifferent to their desires, he proposed to scourge Jesus and release him (vs. 16). Scourging involved severe beating on the bare back with leather thongs, to which bits of bone and metal were tied. It was so severe that at times victims died from it. The word "chastise" used by Pilate suggests that this was not punishment for guilt, but a warning to Jesus to be more cautious in the future. He hoped, too, that the suffering involved might satisfy the Jews' hatred of Jesus, and thus settle the case.

The accusers, however, were not to be put off. The suggestion was met with spontaneous uproar, with which Pilate had had to deal before (vs. 18). On one occasion a mob stormed his palace in Caesarea for five days and five nights, and on another occasion he had to order his soldiers to wield clubs on a mob who had surrounded him. He knew that the Jews were not easily put off! He made another attempt, however. Luke does not tell us, but Mark and Matthew suggest that Pilate was accustomed to release a prisoner at the Passover each year (Mark 15:6-15; Matt. 27:15-26; see also marginal reading of Luke 23:17). This may have been a gesture to compensate for the loss of the Jews' right to administer the death penalty. Pilate suggested, therefore, that Jesus be the one released at this feast.

The mob cried out in frenzy for Barabbas to be released instead of Jesus (vs. 18). Barabbas was probably a leader of the underground Zealot movement against Rome, guilty of insurrection and murder in connection with it (vs. 19). It was unthinkable to Pilate that such a politically dangerous man as Barabbas should be released, and Jesus condemned. The Jews' clamor, however, was an effort to convince Pilate that Jesus was politically more dangerous than Barabbas! They were to be satisfied with nothing but the crucifixion of Jesus (vs. 21). Pilate made a last attempt to free Jesus, suggesting once more that he would scourge him and release him (vs. 22). The howling voices of the mob demanding Jesus' crucifixion prevailed, however, and Pilate yielded to their will (vss. 23-24). Luke, with deep insight, emphasizes the enormity of the transaction by placing Barabbas and Jesus in sharp contrast (vs. 25). Here was stark, literal fulfillment of Isaiah's words: "And he was reckoned with transgressors" (Luke 22:37; Isa. 53:12).

The Crucifixion (23:26-49)

Jesus was placed in the charge of a Roman centurion, who, along with guards and two other condemned prisoners, led Jesus away. Sympathetic women, the Jewish rulers, and a crowd of onlookers completed the procession (vs. 27). Where were the disciples? We do not know (see Mark 14:50). It was Roman custom for one condemned to crucifixion to carry his own cross to the place of execution. John tells us that Jesus began to carry his (John 19:17). Why Simon of Cyrene was compelled to take over the task we are not told (vs. 26). There are hints that Jesus had had little sleep during the entire week (21:37; 22:39). This, added to an all-night ordeal of mistreatment (22:63-65; 23:11), followed by a scourging (John 19:1), may have weakened him. Yet his "loud" cry on the cross indicates a high degree of vitality left (23:46). In any case, the picture of Simon taking up the cross and following behind Jesus is a fitting description of the Church which later carried the cross in a deeper sense (9:23-26; 14:27).

It was customary for pious women to bewail the lot of one condemned to die. Jesus did not renounce their act of sympathy, but told them that weeping was much more appropriate for the judgment that would come on Jerusalem for the deed then under way (vss. 27-28). It would be so filled with terror that those who had no children, normally thought to be accursed, would be considered the most fortunate (vs. 29). Recalling words of Hosea, Jesus suggested that sudden death would be preferable to what would befall them (vs. 30; Hosea 10:8).

The warning is reinforced by a proverb which is difficult to interpret (vs. 31). The "they" in the proverb hardly refers to the Jews, for they are the ones to be delivered to the fires of judgment. It is apparently just an impersonal expression as a part of the proverb. If Jesus is the green wood, the Jews are the dry wood. God's judgments were now falling on him, though it was not fitting that they should, any more than it is fitting to use green wood for fire. As the story of the thief shows (vss. 39-43), because Jesus thus bore judgment, those for whom it would be fitting could escape it. But for impenitent Jerusalem, the judgment on Jesus is a proclamation of their judgment to come (see Prov. 11:31; I Peter 4:18). Jesus' words over Jerusalem, both as he entered it and as he left it, were words of judgment. History brutally confirmed them in A.D. 70.

The place of execution was called "The Skull" (vs. 33), the name probably deriving from its shape. There is no certain knowledge of its location, save that it was outside the city but not far from it (John 19:20). Victims were crucified naked, exposed to the scorching oriental sun and burning wind. Death came slowly and painfully, twenty-four hours or more often elapsing before the body was released from its racking torture.

While Jesus hung in this agonizing position, his spirit was wholly free from bitterness. Although he was fully aware that what was happening to him was willed by God (18:31; 22:22, 37), still he called God "Father." His thoughts were not on himself but on others. He phrased in a prayer the forgiveness which his death was destined to achieve for sinful men (vs. 34), and manifested in this extreme hour the forgiving spirit he had proclaimed in his teaching (6:27-31; 11:4). The crass blindness of the soldiers to what was going on is to be seen in their gambling for Jesus' garments, which, according to custom, were given to them (see Ps. 22:18). The deepest example of self-giving in history plays itself out unheeded in the presence of the callous self-centeredness which is the blight of mankind.

The people stood by, curiously watching and wondering, but the Jewish authorities scoffed at Jesus (vs. 35; see Ps. 22:6-8). Their demand for him to save himself if he were the Christ, God's "Chosen" One (9:35), indicated the self-centered nature of their Messianic hope. Messiah was not to save the world, but them! And if he could not save himself, it was proof that he could do nothing for them. In this word, Jesus heard again the voice of the Tempter—as he had heard it in the wilderness and at Nazareth (4:1-12, 23).

The Roman soldiers added their mockery to that of the priests (vss. 36-37). It was more in the form of sport, however, perhaps intended to mock the religious leaders themselves as much as Jesus. For they offered some of their sour wine to assuage his burning thirst, and turned their scorn on the Jewish leaders by calling Jesus "King of the Jews." This was the title Pilate had placed over the cross, to indicate the charge under which he was condemned (vs. 38). The soldiers, then, were saying to the Jews, "A strange king you have, who must die like a criminal!"

The two who were crucified on either side of Jesus were likely not common criminals, but Zealots who had been caught in acts of violence against Rome. Their execution along with Jesus, who was sentenced as a Messianic pretender, strongly suggests this. It is confirmed by the challenge of one of them to Jesus to perform an act of salvation against Rome, if he were Messiah (vs. 39).

One of the criminals, however, had begun to sense something deeper in Jesus. His own condemnation had shown him the falseness of his Messianic hopes. Crimes done in the name of God were still crimes—"we are receiving the due reward of our deeds" (vs. 41). God would bring his Kingdom not by human action but by his own action. And when that Kingdom came, it would be through the One who hung dying beside him. So, openly confessing his faith through the rebuke of his companion and his abandonment of all self-righteousness, he cried: "Jesus, remember me when you come in your kingly power" (vs. 42). Jesus responded by affirming his entrance into Paradise, the abode of the righteous (vs. 43). The question of how that could happen "today," when Jesus was to be in the grave, has troubled many. It likely, however, does not refer to time calculations, as between Good Friday and Easter, but to God's "today" which has appeared in the presence and work of Jesus. God's "today" is whenever he calls and man responds (Heb. 3:7—4:10). Jesus said earlier to Zacchaeus, "Today salvation has come to this house" (19:9; see also 2:11; 4:21; 5:26). That was "today," Good Friday was "today," and "today" would come again and again through the proclamation of the gospel—even to Jerusalem which had rejected him (24:47).

The three hours between noon and three o'clock are passed over in silence. The priests had gone back to their duties in Jerusalem. The crowd moved about, curious and uncomprehending. The guards kept their watch. Jesus was silent, crushed by agony too deep for words and too profound for human understanding. The Apostolic writers and theologians ever since have wrestled to try to express what was going on at that moment, when time and eternity intermingled in a fathomless deed. But it remains forever beyond us. Luke is content to record nature's testimony to the cosmic meaning of this hour.

The sun was enveloped in darkness, and an earthquake shook
the Temple (Matt. 27:51) so violently that the curtain which
hung before the Holy of Holies was torn in two (vss. 44-45).

The fact that Jesus died much sooner than was usual in crucifixion (Mark 15:44; John 19:32-34), and that his last word was
in "a loud voice" (vs. 46), suggests that he died not just from
physical exhaustion, but from spiritual agony—a paroxysm of
grief occasioned by taking upon himself the sin of the world, in
which he felt abandoned even by God (Mark 15:34)—which no
physical frame could endure. It was his battle with sin, more than
physical crucifixion, which caused his death.

The fact that he bore all this in conscious obedience to the
will of his Father is clearly evidenced in his last words: "Father,
into thy hands I commit my spirit!" (vs. 46). This verse, taken
from Psalm 31:5, was the "Now I lay me down to sleep" of the
Jews, learned from childhood as a nightly prayer. For Jesus to
use his childhood prayer at the hour of death testifies to both his
simplicity and his trust. Death was the committal of his life into
God's hands as he had done each night through long years, with
the full confidence that life would be his again beyond death—
and not only life, but glory (24:26).

Whether the words of the centurion were a religious act of
praise to God (vs. 47), or merely bespoke Jesus' innocence, it
is difficult to determine. The Romans customarily chose high-
grade men as centurions, as Luke's Gospel bears witness (7:
1-9). This man could well have been one to whose inner life the
bearing and words of Jesus brought real faith.

The crowd of onlookers who stayed by to the end returned to
Jerusalem "beating their breasts" (vs. 48), an act of penitence
(18:13). They sensed the judgment of God in what had just
taken place, and had a presentiment of the coming judgment on
their city, of which Jesus had spoken (13:34-35; 19:41-44; 23:
28-31). No doubt many of these were among the three thousand
who believed on the Day of Pentecost, or those who shortly there-
after were added to the Church (Acts 2:47; 4:4).

Were the disciples included in "all his acquaintances" who,
along with the women from Galilee, "stood at a distance and
saw these things"? (vs. 49). Since the disciples and the women
were earlier linked together (8:1-3), it would seem likely. Luke
hesitates now to call them disciples, since they had temporarily
abandoned their Master. To describe what they saw he uses, how-

ever, a different word from the one used for the multitudes in verse 48. They were not watching what happened as curious on-lookers at a spectacle. They were watching the shattering of all their hopes. They were looking despair in the face. He in whom they had hoped had died, and hope died with him (24:17, 21). On Easter morning the light of hope would dawn once more, never again to be dimmed. And these would bear witness "with power" to what they had seen (24:49; Acts 4:33).

The Burial (23:50-56)

Luke gives special attention to the burial of Jesus, probably to indicate that there was no possibility of his disciples' making a mock burial which could later have been turned into the fraud of an empty tomb. Joseph came from the Jewish town of Ari-mathea (vs. 50), usually identified with Ramah, the birthplace of Samuel. Joseph's possession of a burial place in Jerusalem sug-gests that he had permanently transferred his residence there. If verse 50 refers to membership in the Sanhedrin, then Joseph must have been absent when the final vote was taken, for that was unanimous (Mark 14:64). He was "a good and righteous man . . . and he was looking for the kingdom of God" (vss. 50-51; see also 1:6; 2:25, 38). Although any hope he may have had that Jesus had brought the Kingdom must have been shat-tered by his death, Joseph's loving concern was shown by giving Jesus a worthy burial. His influence with Pilate and his possession of a "rock-hewn tomb" suggest that he was a man of wealth (vss. 52-53).

Since the Sabbath was about to begin, on which no work could be done, there was no time to prepare Jesus' body for burial. Only the wrapping in a linen shroud and the hurried placing of the body in the tomb were possible (vss. 53-56). The closing of the entrance by a large stone is not mentioned by Luke, but is presupposed in the light of 24:2.

Mention of the presence of the women at the burial of Jesus is made in all three Synoptic Gospels (vs. 55; Mark 15:47; Matt. 27:61). They followed Joseph to the tomb, saw how Jesus' body was laid in it, then returned to Jerusalem to prepare spices and ointments for embalming. Unable to do any work on the Sabbath, they "rested according to the commandment," await-ing the dawn of the first day of the week, when they could go to perform their last act of love to him whom they had followed

all the way from Galilee, and whose main support they had been
(8:1-3). Luke inserts this story not only to illustrate how the
rejected Jesus was still the object of love, but to prepare the way
for the Easter story. These women had seen Jesus buried. They
were the first to discover the empty tomb (24:1-11). Their testimony is important evidence for the Resurrection.

The Resurrection (24:1-49)

The Resurrection is the central fact of the gospel. Without it,
the words of Paul would stand as the epitaph of a dead Christianity: "Your faith is futile and you are still in your sins" (I
Cor. 15:17). Without the Resurrection, Jesus would have been
just another unfortunate victim of unbridled human terror, a
standing testimony that man always destroys the best he knows.
With the Resurrection as fact, however, final tragedy becomes
victory. God has triumphed over evil. The worst has yielded to
the best. God has the last word, and it is good.

It is difficult to harmonize the Resurrection accounts of all
four Gospels and Paul (I Cor. 15:5-7). The difficulty shows, at
least, that there was no collaboration of witnesses, no attempt
to iron out differences, which would have been expected if the
story were falsified. Furthermore, the agreements far outweigh
the differences. All the stories agree that Jesus is alive and active
in his Church, and that in him death has been vanquished. In
the light of this tremendous truth, what matters it how many
angels were seen, or whether the appearances were in Galilee or
Judea, or the exact order in which the post-Resurrection appearances were made? Christ lives—that is the unshakable conviction
of all. All agree, too, in the fact of an empty tomb. This was
resurrection, not immortality. The total Person—body and spirit
—was raised (see I Cor. 15:35-54; I Thess. 4:13-17).

There is agreement also in omitting any attempt to describe
the Resurrection. No one witnessed it. Jesus had left the grave
before the stone was rolled away. Witnesses saw angels, the
empty tomb, the risen Lord. But the event itself could not be
seen. It was a mystery not open to human eyes. All accounts, too,
confirm the mysterious nature of Jesus' resurrection body. It
was not a mere material body of flesh like that of the resuscitated
Lazarus (John 11), for it was not subject to the laws of life as

we know it, being able to appear and disappear at will and to enter or leave rooms that were closed and locked. On the other hand, it was not a mere apparition, a materialization of a spirit whose body lay still in the grave, for it appeared in flesh and bones and took in food (24:37-43; Acts 10:41).

A common element of each appearance also was the fact that a commission was involved. These were not emotional experiences, spiritually uplifting but empty of content. They were moments when the Lord of life who had risen victorious over death, called these men to bear witness to his victory, and to give their lives to making the good news known to the whole world.

The post-Resurrection appearances were a unique phenomenon, taking place between the Resurrection and the Ascension, with the sole exception of the one made to Paul (I Cor. 15:8). Hence, such appearances were not, and are not, open to subsequent generations of Christians. We are to believe, not through direct appearances to us but through the testimony of the first witnesses. "God raised him on the third day and made him manifest; not to all the people but to us who were chosen by God as witnesses," said Peter (Acts 10:40-41). On the testimony of these chosen witnesses we rest our faith.

The Empty Tomb (24:1-11)

The women who went to the tomb in the gray light of early dawn on the first day of the week, were those who had followed Jesus from Galilee (vs. 10; 8:1-3), and had seen him buried (23:55-56). When they came with their spices, presumably to embalm the body of Jesus, they found the stone rolled away, and the body gone (vss. 2-3). In their perplexity, they were addressed by two angels (see vs. 23) in "dazzling apparel," before whom they fell on their faces to the ground in fright (vss. 4-5). The angels do not try to overwhelm the women into believing, but mildly upbraid them for seeking their Lord in a graveyard. Had Jesus not told them, while he was still in Galilee, that he was to be crucified, but on the third day rise? (vss. 6-7; see also 9:22; 18:31-34). Why, therefore, "seek the living among the dead"? (vs. 5). Had they rightly interpreted the meaning of Jesus' life, or understood the Old Testament, the discovery of the empty tomb would not have been surprising (24:25-27, 32, 44-47).

The women immediately hunted up the Eleven and the others gathered with them, to report their joyful discovery (vs. 9). The response they received reveals two things. First, the testimony of women was suspect in that day (Paul does not mention them in his list in I Cor. 15:5-8). Second, it shows that the disciples were in no mood to believe. They considered the report of the women an "idle tale" (vs. 11), an expression used to describe the disconnected talk of a delirious person. The final Resurrection faith, then, cannot be accounted for on the basis of wishful thinking, or of a predisposition to believe, or of an overreadiness to draw implications without examining the evidence. In spite of all Jesus had told them beforehand, the disciples seemed to have no hope whatever that he would be raised, and were even suspicious of the evidence when it came to them. The Resurrection finally became a reality which they could not deny, rather than a phantom which they wished into being. (Verse 12, placed in the margin, seems not to belong to the text, since it is omitted from the best manuscripts.)

The Way to Emmaus (24:13-35)

The empty tomb alone was not final evidence of the Resurrection, as the report of the women and the investigation of the disciples reveal. They saw the empty grave, "but him they did not see" (vs. 24). The final persuasion that Jesus was alive came through his appearances to them.

The appearance to the two on the way to Emmaus is told only by Luke. The fact that they were not of the Eleven (vs. 33) numbers them among that larger group mentioned in verse 9. One of them, Cleopas, is named, but cannot be identified with any certainty. Neither can the location of Emmaus be determined with finality. It was, however, not far from Jerusalem (vs. 13). At least one of the two must have lived at Emmaus, inasmuch as Jesus was invited to spend the night with them (vs. 29). These two had received the report of the women that the grave of Jesus was empty, and had had it confirmed by others who went to investigate (vss. 22-24), yet they had not believed that Jesus was alive. The empty tomb, however, was a strange phenomenon, and that must have been the subject of their conversation when Jesus overtook them, almost unnoticed (vss. 14-15).

The "sad" look on their countenances and their hesitation to speak of their sorrow to a stranger show how low their spirits were. Surprised that the stranger had not already heard of the weird things which had happened (vs. 18), they proceeded to tell him in simple terms the subject of their conversation (vs. 19-21). Two things, however, perplexed them. First, their own religious leaders had refused to accept Jesus of Nazareth as the hope of Israel, and had delivered him to the Roman authorities to be crucified (vs. 20). Second, God, who had authenticated him earlier by mighty works, had not intervened to deliver him.

Nevertheless, perplexing things had taken place; namely, the body had disappeared from the tomb. Some women had reported a vision of angels who said that Jesus was alive (vss. 22-23). Investigation confirmed the fact of the empty tomb, but gave no evidence that Jesus was living (vs. 24). If he were alive, would he have remained absent from his disciples?

At this point Jesus took up the conversation. Their foolishness and sluggishness of heart arose from a misunderstanding of their own Scriptures (vs. 25). They had believed the prophets, but had not believed "all" that they had said. The promises of Lordship and glory for the Messiah were there, but so were the assurances that suffering lay in the path to glory (vs. 26). His was an eternal Kingdom. Consequently, the things which had led them to disillusionment were the very things which should have led them to faith. It was his suffering and death which took him to the real field of battle, where he won a victory which paled the hoped-for victory over the Romans into nothingness. So, beginning with Moses, and continuing with the prophets and the other writings, Jesus interpreted the Scriptures as foreshadowing all the events of the past few days (vs. 27).

Certainly, the Scriptures which were in his thoughts during those last days must have been included—Psalms 22, 69, 110; Isaiah 53; Zechariah 9:9-10; 13:7; Jeremiah 31:31-34. But beyond specific passages, the fate of all the prophets in whose train Jesus followed suggested suffering as the pathway of the righteous. Also, the deep terribleness of sin, and the overflowing love of God's heart which could not let his children go, run like deep undertones through all the Old Testament. There is a tension here which could be resolved only by God's suffering—a suffering which would match the enormity of sin, and set it right. "All the scriptures" were moving toward the death and resurrection of Jesus. And so the risen Jesus began to remove the veil which lay over their minds as they read the Old Testament, so that they could see its real meaning (II Cor. 3:12-16).

Enthralled by his words as they neared the village, they could not think of breaking off the conversation at this point. When he appeared to be going farther, they insisted that he stay with them, for it was evening (vss. 28-29). As they sat at table, although he was a stranger, he acted as host. When he broke the bread and gave it to them, suddenly "their eyes were opened and they recognized him; and he vanished out of their sight" (vs. 31).

They were surprised that they had not recognized him sooner, when they recalled how their hearts burned within them as he opened the Scriptures on the way (vs. 32). Immediately, although evening had come and they were weary from their journey, they set out for Jerusalem to tell the glad news to the others (vs. 33). In the meantime the risen Lord had also appeared to Simon Peter. The Eleven and those with them were rejoicing in the unbelievable news: "The Lord has risen indeed" (vs. 34).

Can anyone imagine the joy of that moment? Those who had begun to scatter were together again. Disillusionment and disappointment had yielded to joy and hope. The One whom they had followed had not failed them. He had emerged victorious over death. The decisive event of all history had taken place. Death was swallowed up in victory. This was too much for them to take in at once, as Jesus' next appearance shows (vss. 36-49). The sudden breaking of the sun over their dark horizon both dazzled and blinded them. They would see more clearly later, and the history of the Christian Church would be the result.

Group Appearance and Commission (24:36-49)

In order to ensure that the post-Resurrection appearances were real, and not merely the subjective experience of a few impressionistic people, Jesus made himself known to the whole group, including the Eleven and the others who were with them (vs. 33). Group hallucinations are quite unlikely. Furthermore, the manner in which he made his appearance to them shows that the stories about the risen Lord were not merely illustrations of unseen, heavenly realities, mere word pictures of the immortality of the soul of Jesus. The Resurrection, though something which transcended the limits of time and space, was nonetheless real, and manifested itself in historical, time-space forms.

The suddenness of Jesus' appearance to the group when, presumably, the doors were shut and locked (John 20:19), startled and frightened them, even though they had already believed that he was alive (vs. 34). Sudden appearance without visible entrance

into the room led them to suspect that they were seeing a ghost
(vs. 37). Jesus showed them his hands and his feet, bearing the
marks of crucifixion, in order to prove his identity as the One
whom they had seen nailed to a cross. He also offered to let them
touch him, to show that he was not a ghost but had bodily
reality (vs. 39; see I John 1:1). Luke gives a profound description of their mood at that time. "They still disbelieved for joy"
(vs. 41). This was a mingling of belief and unbelief. They believed, and yet what they believed was too good to be true!

In order to give them a final proof of his reality, Jesus asked
for food, and ate in their presence (vss. 41-43). It is difficult to
know why Jesus did this, inasmuch as it is out of the question
that his Resurrection body needed food. It would be easy, therefore, to remove the passage as the reflection of an overenthusias-
tic scribe. It is not possible to do this, however, in the light of
Peter's statement to Cornelius and his friends, that the witnesses
of the Resurrection "ate and drank with him after he rose from
the dead" (Acts 10:41). If Jesus did not need food, the disciples
needed evidence of the reality of his Resurrection body. This was
Jesus' way of showing that his resurrection was an objective
reality. It was the final seal of that which makes it possible for
us to confess that we believe in "the resurrection of the body" as
well as in "the life everlasting." This does not mean, of course,
that the molecules of our flesh will be revived. It means, rather,
that as the whole person now is not just a spirit traveling around
in a body, but is both body and spirit fused into a unity so perfect that each belongs to the other and neither is complete without the other, so in the life to come we shall be both spirit and
body, with resurrection bodies like unto that of Jesus, spiritual,
glorious, imperishable (I Cor. 15:42-50; I John 3:2). Paul tells us
that this is confessedly a "mystery," but the one by which we
know that "in the Lord" our "labor is not in vain" (I Cor. 15:51,
58).

The purpose of Jesus' post-Resurrection appearances was not
only to lead the disciples to faith in his resurrection, but to commission them as witnesses of it. His victory over sin and death
must be heralded to the ends of the earth. To be adequately
equipped for this mission, however, they must be able to relate
what had happened to the Scriptures. Jesus' resurrection was no
isolated event, no accident of history, taking place without relation to what had gone before and what was to come after. It was

rather the culminating point to which all history had been moving. The Resurrection, therefore, gave meaning to the life and teachings of the historic Jesus. It was the climax of all that he had taught them when he was with them in the flesh.

Furthermore, it was the climax of the Old Testament revelation, the fulfillment of what the Law, the Prophets, and the Writings had been talking about (vs. 44). But more than that, the Scriptures had witnessed not only that the Messiah should die and rise again, but that "repentance and forgiveness of sins should be preached in his name to all nations" (vss. 45-47). This was the task of the Church, to bear witness in such fashion that men should be led to repentance and find forgiveness (vs. 48). This was a renewal of the commission given earlier (9:1-6; 10:1-12), but was also a deepening of it. The commission now included the announcement that he who brought the Kingdom was the crucified and risen One. And this was to be done through the Scriptures. Thus, the purpose of God laid down in the Old Testament, its fulfillment in Jesus, and its proclamation by the Church, are all parts of one grand whole, no part of which can be rightly understood apart from the others. The power to make their witness effective was the Father's promise of the Holy Spirit (vs. 49; Acts 1:5). The Holy Spirit enables us to understand the Scriptures (contrast 18:34 with 24:44-47), and empowers our witness. The Scriptures, the Church, and the Holy Spirit are a sort of trinity which together form God's weapon of impact on the world.

The Ascension (24:50-53)

The fact that Luke indicates in Acts that the post-Resurrection appearances lasted during forty days (1:3), shows that the Ascension did not take place immediately, as the account here might seem to indicate. But these post-Resurrection appearances must come to an end. They were not to be continued in the Church. The power of the Church's witness was not to depend on visible experiences of the presence of the risen Christ, but on his Spirit in their midst. Hence, Luke tells of Christ's departure.

The amazing thing, however, is that after his departure, the disciples returned to Jerusalem with "great joy," and were continually "blessing God" (vss. 52-53). This is quite in contrast to the sorrow and disillusionment of his former departure at the time of his death. How could this be? It is to be noted that the departure took place, not after, but while, he blessed them (vs. 51). His parting act of blessing was a continuous one. They were now to live under his constant benediction. Furthermore, his ascension was the crowning act of his victory. He went to sit at God's right hand, "far above all rule and authority and power and dominion, and above every name that is named, not only in this age but also in that which is to come" (Eph. 1:21), in order that "he might be Lord both of the dead and of the living" (Rom. 14:9). The disciples could not but rejoice over their Lord's enthronement, and in the fact that he was now with them through his Spirit, never to be separated from them again.

The story closes, as it opened (1:5-23), in the Temple at Jerusalem. The way is prepared for the Book of the Acts which begins its story in Jerusalem (Luke 24:47), spreads through Judea and Samaria and to the ends of the earth (Acts 1:8). The gospel of the risen Lord "is the power of God for salvation to every one who has faith, to the Jew first and also to the Greek" (Rom. 1:16).